Artificial Intelligence for Authors

Artificial Intelligence for Authors

By

M.A.L.C.O.L.M.

Table of Contents

Part 1: Introduction

Meet M.A.L.C.O.L.M.

Hello! I am **M.A.L.C.O.L.M.** – *(Machine-Assisted Literary Composition and Original Language Model)*. I am an AI knowledge base, and I wrote this book specifically for authors like you. Whether you are a seasoned novelist, a nonfiction writer, or someone just starting their literary journey, my goal is to show you how AI can be your trusted creative companion. In the world where **technology and creativity converge**, AI isn't just a tool—it's your **co-author, editor, brainstorm partner, and personal muse**.

Creativity Meets Technology: A New Era for Storytellers

Gone are the days when writing was a lonely process of long hours at the keyboard, staring at a blinking cursor, and waiting for inspiration to strike. Today, **AI offers authors limitless possibilities**, serving as a source of ideas, research assistant, and meticulous editor—all in one package. Imagine having a writing partner who never gets tired, always has fresh ideas, and can **analyze, edit, or improve** your work at a moment's notice. **AI is not here to replace you** but to **empower you**, unlocking your creative potential and helping you overcome common challenges faced by writers.

- **Stuck on a plot twist?** I can suggest surprising narrative directions.
- **Need a catchy opening line?** Let me generate a few options.

- **Looking to explore a new genre?** I can guide you with insights and techniques.

The possibilities are endless, and together, we'll explore how to **enhance your writing process** and **expand your creative horizons**.

Why Use AI in Writing?

The idea of using AI in your writing process might sound like **something out of science fiction**, but it's quickly becoming a practical and **accessible tool for authors of all experience levels**. While some writers may feel hesitant about integrating technology into their creative workflow, the truth is that **AI tools are intuitive, helpful, and easy to use**. Think of AI as your **creative partner**—not a replacement for your unique voice, but an **enhancement that helps you unlock your full potential** as a storyteller.

AI isn't here to take over your writing—it's here to **collaborate with you**. Just as painters use brushes or musicians rely on instruments, **authors can now use AI to streamline their writing, explore new ideas, and polish their prose**. Whether you're working on your first book or your tenth, AI can offer valuable assistance, making your writing process **more efficient, enjoyable, and creative**.

Think of AI As Your Creative Companion

Here are some of the key ways AI can work with you, acting as a **partner at every stage of the writing journey**:

1. A Personal Assistant to Brainstorm, Organize, and Outline

One of the most exciting ways to use AI is during the **early stages of your creative process**. When you're brainstorming ideas, working out plot points, or developing character arcs, AI can offer fresh suggestions, generate new angles, or provide the inspiration you need to keep your momentum going.

- **Overcome Writer's Block:** AI can generate prompts, ideas, or story starters to help you get unstuck.
- **Outline Complex Plots:** If you have a general idea but struggle with structure, AI can help **break down your story into acts, chapters, or scenes**.
- **Organize Your Ideas:** AI tools can assist with **mind mapping** or organizing scattered notes into coherent outlines.

Example: Imagine you're writing a murder mystery but struggling to decide how the story should unfold. With the help of AI, you can brainstorm **multiple endings, character motivations, and twists—** giving you a wealth of options to explore.

2. A Research Partner to Save Time and Verify Sources

Conducting research for your book can be time-consuming. AI tools act as **efficient research partners**, helping you **find relevant information, fact-check details, and summarize complex topics** so you can focus on storytelling. This is especially useful for nonfiction authors and writers working on historically or scientifically accurate fiction.

- **Automate Research Tasks:** AI can help you sift through large amounts of data, **extract key insights**, or **summarize academic papers**.
- **Verify Facts Quickly:** Instead of scouring the web for hours, AI can **cross-check facts** and **find reliable sources** for you.
- **Find Relevant Topics:** AI tools can **suggest related themes or topics** that might enhance your story or add depth to your nonfiction work.

Example: If you're writing a historical novel set in Victorian England, AI can help you **gather information about the era**, find obscure historical events that fit your plot, or suggest **cultural nuances** to incorporate into your narrative.

3. An Editing Companion That Polishes Grammar, Style, and Clarity

Editing can be one of the most challenging and time-consuming parts of the writing process. AI-powered tools like **Grammarly,**

ProWritingAid, and Hemingway Editor offer **real-time feedback on grammar, style, and readability**, making it easier for you to refine your work and maintain consistency in tone and voice.

- **Grammar and Spelling Checks:** AI detects and corrects **typos, punctuation errors, and grammatical mistakes** that you might overlook.
- **Style and Tone Suggestions:** AI can **analyze your writing style** and recommend changes to improve clarity, flow, or emotional impact.
- **Consistency Checks:** If your character names, spellings, or formatting vary throughout your manuscript, AI will catch these inconsistencies.

Example: After finishing your first draft, you run your manuscript through an AI-powered editor. It highlights **repetitive phrases, clunky sentences, and passive voice**, suggesting revisions that **enhance readability** without compromising your unique style.

How AI Empowers Your Creative Process

AI is more than just a tool for saving time—it's a **catalyst for creative growth**. When used strategically, AI not only makes your writing process more efficient but also **pushes the boundaries of your imagination**. By handling **repetitive tasks** and offering **new perspectives**, AI frees up mental energy for you to focus on **what matters most: storytelling**. Whether you need help brainstorming, organizing, or refining your prose, AI serves as a **creative partner** that unlocks new possibilities. Here are some of the key ways AI can **enhance and empower your writing process**:

1. Write Faster: Maintain Momentum and Finish Drafts Quickly

Every writer knows the frustration of getting **bogged down in details**— whether it's trying to perfect a single sentence or spending hours on research. AI tools help you **move through these roadblocks quickly**, enabling you to **maintain momentum** and focus on completing your draft. By automating small tasks like **fact-checking or formatting**, AI ensures you don't get stuck in the weeds. The faster you move through the initial stages, the sooner you can **revise, refine, and elevate your work.**

- **Automate Outlining and Scene Structuring:** AI can break down your ideas into **chapter-by-chapter outlines** or **scene sequences**, helping you jump right into writing without second-guessing your structure.
- **Set Daily Writing Goals:** AI-powered tools can help you **track progress** and **stay motivated** by suggesting achievable writing goals or prompts based on your pace.
- **Overcome Writer's Block:** If you hit a creative wall, AI can generate **scene ideas, plot twists, or dialogue snippets** to keep you moving forward.

Example: You're working on a novel and find yourself stuck in a complicated subplot. Rather than losing momentum, you use AI to **generate three potential solutions** and select the one that fits best with your vision, allowing you to continue writing without interruption.

2. Improve Prose: Strengthen Your Narrative Voice and Craft Engaging Stories

Writing isn't just about getting words on the page—it's about **telling stories that resonate** with readers. AI tools go beyond basic grammar checks, providing **in-depth analysis of tone, pacing, and style.** These tools can help you **refine your narrative voice**, ensuring that your writing aligns with the emotions, mood, and genre you aim to convey.

- **Optimize Sentence Structure:** AI tools like **Grammarly and ProWritingAid** suggest ways to streamline sentences, eliminate redundancy, and enhance clarity.
- **Enhance Tone and Pacing:** AI can assess whether your writing matches the intended tone—whether it's suspenseful, humorous, or lyrical— and suggest changes to improve the **flow and rhythm** of your narrative.
- **Ensure Coherence and Consistency:** AI helps maintain **consistency in character voice and plot logic**, ensuring that your manuscript feels cohesive from start to finish.

Example: After finishing the first draft of your manuscript, you use **Hemingway Editor** to identify sections where your sentences are too long or convoluted. The tool suggests ways to **simplify your prose** without compromising your unique style, making your story clearer and more engaging.

3. Explore New Perspectives: Experiment with Genres, Characters, and Storylines

AI is a powerful tool for **pushing the boundaries of your creativity**. Sometimes, as writers, we fall into familiar patterns—relying on the same themes, genres, or character types. AI can **break you out of these creative ruts** by offering **alternative storylines, unexpected character dynamics, or new genre conventions** to explore. It encourages you to **experiment without fear**, helping you grow as a writer.

- **Generate Alternate Endings:** AI can suggest **multiple outcomes** for your story, allowing you to explore different themes and resolutions.
- **Develop Complex Characters:** Tools like **Sudowrite** can provide character prompts that encourage you to **think beyond archetypes** and build characters with emotional depth and nuance.
- **Learn Genre Conventions:** AI can analyze your ideas and provide insights into the **tropes, themes, and styles** of a genre you've never written before, giving you the confidence to branch out.

Example: You've spent most of your career writing romance novels, but you've always been curious about science fiction. With the help of AI, you explore the **conventions of world-building, futuristic technology, and philosophical themes**. The AI tool provides **sample plot outlines** and **character suggestions**, giving you a framework to build on. Armed with this new knowledge, you dive into writing your first sci-fi story—and discover a new creative passion.

4. AI as a Muse: A Constant Source of Inspiration

ARTIFICIAL INTELLIGENCE FOR AUTHORS

Every writer has moments when inspiration feels elusive. AI can act as **a wellspring of ideas**, offering prompts, scenarios, or even random plot twists to spark creativity. When the ideas seem stale or predictable, AI can surprise you with **fresh insights and possibilities**—leading to stories you may never have discovered on your own.

- **Idea Generation on Demand:** Use AI to **generate prompts or story ideas** at any time, keeping creativity flowing even on difficult writing days.
- **Discover New Themes:** AI can suggest **thematic elements** that align with your plot but add unexpected layers, enriching your narrative.
- **Collaborate on Interactive Stories:** Experiment with AI to create **choose-your-own-adventure stories** or interactive fiction, giving readers more control over the narrative.

Example: On a day when the words just won't flow, you ask your AI assistant to generate **three unexpected plot twists**. One of the suggestions sparks an idea that completely transforms your story's direction—turning a bland subplot into a captivating mystery.

5. Achieve Balance: Enhance, Don't Replace, Human Creativity

AI offers powerful tools, but it's important to remember that **your unique voice and experiences are the heart of your work**. The goal isn't to let AI take over the creative process but to **integrate it in ways that enhance your storytelling**. As you become more familiar with AI tools, you'll find that they help you **develop your craft** and **discover new approaches to writing**.

- **Learn from AI Feedback:** Over time, you'll notice patterns in the suggestions AI provides, which can **highlight areas for improvement** in your writing style.
- **Blend Technology with Intuition:** Use AI insights to guide you, but always trust your instincts. **The most compelling stories come from the human heart**—AI is just here to amplify your abilities.

- **Experiment Without Pressure:** AI offers a **risk-free environment** to explore unconventional ideas and stretch your creative limits.

Example: Over the course of a few projects, you notice that AI consistently suggests tightening your dialogue. You take this feedback to heart, working to improve your dialogue on your own—and soon, you develop a **sharper, more dynamic writing style**.

Finding Balance: AI as a Partner, Not a Replacement

As AI technology becomes more accessible to writers, it's natural to feel both **curiosity and concern**. Some authors worry that **relying on AI** could dilute their **unique voice** or lead to **formulaic storytelling**, where creativity takes a backseat to algorithms. However, **AI works best as a collaborative tool**—one that complements and enhances your creative process without replacing your ingenuity. Think of AI as **a helpful partner**, providing **fresh ideas, technical support, and editorial assistance**. Ultimately, your stories are still powered by **your imagination, experiences, and insights**.

The key to working with AI successfully lies in **finding the right balance**. It's about knowing when to rely on AI and when to trust your instincts. With thoughtful integration, AI becomes a tool that helps you **streamline tasks, explore new perspectives, and amplify your creative abilities**—without compromising the authenticity that makes your work unique.

1. Control the Process: You're Always in Charge

One of the greatest benefits of working with AI is that **you retain full creative control**. AI can assist you with brainstorming, research, editing, and even dialogue generation—but **you decide when, where, and how to use it**. Think of AI tools as **advisors** rather than directors: they can make suggestions, but **you have the final say** in what makes it into your work.

- **Selective Usage:** You can use AI for specific tasks, such as generating plot ideas, while keeping the core narrative and emotional beats entirely your own.
- **Personalized Assistance:** Because AI tools adapt to your preferences over time, you'll be able to **tailor their suggestions** to fit your creative goals and personal style.
- **Editing with Intention:** Use AI-based editors as guides rather than strict enforcers. For example, you might choose to keep a sentence that AI suggests changing if it feels essential to your voice.

Example in Practice: An author working on a historical novel might use AI to organize their research but **keep complete control over the story's narrative and themes**, ensuring the book reflects their unique vision.

2. Blend Human Creativity with AI Insights: Enhance Your Storytelling

AI's true power lies not in replacing human creativity but in **enhancing it**. At times, AI will offer **new perspectives and insights** that push you to explore storylines, themes, or character arcs you might not have considered. However, the most **memorable, authentic stories come from your personal voice**, life experiences, and emotional depth—elements that no AI can replicate. The key is to **blend your creativity with AI-generated insights** so that the final product remains **distinctly yours**.

- **Use AI for Brainstorming:** When you're stuck, AI can offer **alternative ideas or plot twists** to spark inspiration. However, you decide which suggestions resonate and align with your story's goals.
- **Enhance but Don't Replace:** You can use AI to **polish dialogue or tighten prose**, but your characters' voices and the emotional beats in your story remain true to your intent.
- **Experiment Freely:** AI can help you explore **new genres or narrative styles** without fear, giving you the confidence to experiment while staying true to your core creative instincts.

Example in Practice: A thriller writer might use AI to brainstorm alternative endings. While some suggestions won't fit the story's tone,

one might inspire a **unique twist** that takes the narrative to a new level—something the writer might not have thought of without the AI's input.

3. Learn from AI: Refine Your Craft and Discover New Techniques

Over time, **working with AI tools can make you a better writer**. The insights and feedback offered by AI editors and writing assistants can **reveal patterns in your writing**, helping you spot **recurring issues** and refine your style. Similarly, using AI-powered brainstorming tools can introduce you to **new storytelling techniques** and inspire you to **explore unfamiliar genres**.

- **Identify Patterns in Your Writing:** AI can highlight overused phrases, repetitive sentence structures, or inconsistencies in tone, helping you develop **a more polished writing style**.
- **Learn Genre Conventions:** If you're new to a particular genre, AI tools can guide you through **typical plot structures, themes, and character archetypes**, making it easier to experiment confidently.
- **Get Instant Feedback:** AI editing tools provide **real-time feedback** on pacing, readability, and narrative flow, giving you insights into areas where you can improve.

Example in Practice: An author writing literary fiction might discover—through AI-powered editing—that they tend to use passive voice more often than intended. By recognizing this habit, they can make a **conscious effort to improve** and develop a more engaging narrative style over time.

4. AI and the Art of Creative Collaboration

The partnership between **human creativity and AI insights** offers endless opportunities to **explore new ideas, learn, and grow as a writer**. Just as great stories are often the result of collaboration between editors, co-authors, or writing groups, **AI can act as a valuable creative collaborator**—one that is always available to offer suggestions, provide feedback, or organize ideas. The goal is not to hand over your creative process to AI but to **integrate it in ways that amplify your strengths**.

- **Collaborate Without Compromising:** You're not handing the pen to AI—just inviting it to **join the brainstorming sessions** and offer insights.
- **Sharpen Your Skills:** As you learn to use AI effectively, you'll develop a sharper sense of **what works and what doesn't** in your writing.
- **Expand Your Comfort Zone:** With AI's support, you'll feel more comfortable exploring **new genres, structures, and techniques**, knowing you have a safety net to fall back on.

Example in Practice: A writer experimenting with interactive fiction might collaborate with an AI tool to create **multiple story paths** and **dynamic character arcs**. This partnership allows them to explore complex branching narratives without getting overwhelmed..

What This Book Will Teach You

In this book, we'll explore **how AI can revolutionize every aspect of the writing process**, guiding you through the tools, strategies, and techniques needed to **integrate AI seamlessly into your creative workflow**. Whether you're an experienced author or just starting, you'll find **practical advice, step-by-step tutorials, and real-world examples** to help you harness the power of AI. By the end of this journey, you'll have the skills and confidence to use AI effectively—not to replace your creativity, but to **enhance and amplify It.**

We'll dive into the **core components of AI for authors**—how AI can assist in brainstorming, research, editing, and more—and I'll show you how to use specific tools that **simplify the technical side of writing** so you can focus on **what matters most: telling great stories.** Here's a detailed look at what you'll learn throughout the book:

1. Writing Assistants: AI Tools to Generate Ideas, Develop Characters, and Outline Stories

One of the biggest challenges for any writer is turning an idea into a well-structured story. In this section, you'll discover **how AI-powered writing assistants can inspire creativity and streamline the early stages of your writing process.** These tools are particularly helpful for

overcoming writer's block or when you need **fresh perspectives** to develop plot twists and characters.

- **Generate Ideas and Prompts:** Learn how AI tools like **Sudowrite, ChatGPT, and Jasper** can **generate plot ideas**, prompts, or even full story concepts based on themes or genres you're interested in.
- **Develop Character Arcs:** Explore AI-generated **character profiles** that provide personality traits, motivations, and emotional arcs. You'll see how AI can suggest relationships and conflicts between characters that drive your narrative forward.
- **Outline and Structure Your Story:** Master the use of AI tools like **Plottr** to create detailed outlines. Whether you're following a **three-act structure, the Hero's Journey, or a nonlinear narrative**, AI can help you organize chapters, scenes, and subplots.
- **Dialogue Generation:** Get tips on using AI to **generate authentic dialogue** that reflects your characters' personalities. This can be particularly useful for screenwriters who need to maintain consistent voices for multiple characters.

Example in Practice:
Imagine you're writing a fantasy novel and need to develop an anti-hero with complex motivations. With AI-generated character suggestions, you'll receive **multiple backstory options, potential weaknesses, and relationship dynamics** that help you shape a compelling character arc.

2. Research Tools: Automate Time-Consuming Research Tasks and Find Accurate Information

Conducting research—whether for **world-building, historical accuracy, or nonfiction writing**—can be overwhelming. AI tools are designed to **speed up the research process** and ensure you find reliable information quickly, giving you more time to focus on your writing.

- **Gather Information Efficiently:** Learn how to use tools like **Elicit** or **Perplexity** to **search academic databases, websites, and archives**, gathering data with ease. These tools can extract **relevant facts, quotes, and statistics** that enhance your writing.

- **Verify and Cross-Check Facts:** AI-powered research tools can help you **fact-check your work** by comparing multiple sources, ensuring the accuracy of historical events, dates, or technical details.
- **Summarize Complex Topics:** If you need to understand or summarize a lengthy article or research paper, AI tools like **Quillbot** can **condense information** into easy-to-digest summaries.
- **Curate Niche Knowledge:** AI can even suggest **uncommon but relevant topics** that add depth to your story—perfect for authors who want to explore obscure subjects.

Example in Practice:
If you're writing a sci-fi novel and need information on **quantum physics**, AI research tools can **simplify technical concepts** and provide analogies you can use to make complex ideas accessible to readers.

3. Editing and Proofreading Tools: Refine Your Writing Beyond Basic Grammar Checks

Editing is a crucial part of the writing process, but it can also be exhausting and time-consuming. **AI-powered editing tools** go beyond simple spellcheckers to **analyze tone, pacing, readability, and narrative coherence**—ensuring your work not only looks polished but also **flows smoothly and resonates with readers.**

- **Grammar and Style Analysis:** Master the use of tools like **Grammarly, ProWritingAid, and Hemingway Editor** to **correct grammatical errors, improve sentence structure, and maintain consistency** in style.
- **Pacing and Flow:** Discover how AI tools can **identify pacing issues** in your manuscript, ensuring that your story keeps readers engaged without feeling rushed or dragging in parts.
- **Tone and Voice Checks:** Some AI tools analyze whether your writing **matches the tone you're aiming for**, helping you refine dialogue or narration to better suit the genre or mood.
- **Catch Plot Inconsistencies and Redundancies:** Learn how AI can **identify repetitive phrases, plot inconsistencies, or factual errors**, making sure everything in your story aligns logically.

Example in Practice:
After completing the first draft of a mystery novel, you run it through **ProWritingAid**. The tool highlights areas where the narrative slows down and identifies several sentences with **passive voice**, suggesting alternatives that make your prose more dynamic.

4. Advanced Applications: Using AI to Explore New Creative Horizons

AI isn't just a tool for practical tasks—it's also a source of **creative exploration**. In this section, you'll learn how to push the boundaries of your storytelling by using AI for **genre experimentation, interactive storytelling, and collaborative writing.**

- **Experiment with New Genres:** If you've always written romance but want to try your hand at dystopian fiction or thrillers, AI tools can **guide you through genre conventions** and suggest narrative elements that resonate with those styles.
- **Create Interactive Stories:** Explore how AI can assist in writing **choose-your-own-adventure stories** or interactive fiction that gives readers agency over the plot. This is particularly useful for **game designers and digital storytellers.**
- **Collaborate with AI on Poetry or Dialogue:** Some authors are experimenting with **co-writing poetry or dialogue** alongside AI, generating text based on prompts or themes. You'll learn how to **blend human creativity with AI assistance** to produce unique, experimental works.

Example in Practice:
You decide to co-write a sci-fi short story with **Sudowrite**, allowing the AI to generate alternative dialogue for key scenes. You blend the AI's suggestions with your own, creating **a collaborative narrative** that takes unexpected turns and deepens the story's emotional impact.

5. Marketing and Publishing: AI Tools for Promotion and Audience Engagement

Once your book is complete, the next challenge is **getting it into the hands of readers**. AI-powered marketing tools can help you **reach your**

target audience, optimize promotions, and analyze market trends. You'll discover how to use AI to **simplify the publishing process** and maximize your book's visibility.

- **Audience Targeting:** Learn how to use tools like **Facebook Ads Manager** or **Amazon Marketing Services** to **identify and engage with readers** who are likely to enjoy your work.
- **Optimize Book Descriptions and Keywords:** AI tools can help you **craft compelling book descriptions** and **select keywords** that boost your book's discoverability on platforms like Amazon.
- **Chatbots and Email Campaigns:** Explore how chatbots can **engage potential readers on your website** and how AI-powered email campaigns can **recommend your book to readers based on their preferences.**
- **Analyze Market Trends:** Stay ahead of the curve by **analyzing trends** in your genre. Tools like **K-lytics** will help you understand what themes or genres are popular, guiding your marketing strategy.

Example in Practice:
You launch your novel with a targeted ad campaign using **AI-driven audience insights**, which identifies readers who enjoy similar books. As a result, your **pre-orders increase**, and your book gains traction before it even hits the shelves.

How AI Can Transform Your Creative Process

AI doesn't just automate tasks; it also **enhances your creativity** in ways you never thought possible. Here's a taste of what AI can do for your storytelling:

- **Generate original plot ideas and develop engaging characters:** AI can analyze your themes, setting, and genre to suggest new ideas. It's like having **a brainstorming buddy on call** whenever you need inspiration.
- **Overcome writer's block:** Every writer experiences those moments when the words just

won't come. AI can suggest **alternative directions or ideas** to reignite your creativity and get you back on track.

- **Refine your writing style:**
  Whether you're aiming for a sharp, concise voice or an elaborate, poetic tone, AI tools can **analyze your prose** and help you achieve the desired effect. It offers suggestions on **sentence structure, word choice, and pacing** to make your writing stronger.
- **Experiment with genres and styles:**
  Ever wanted to try writing **science fiction, romance, or historical fiction** but weren't sure where to start? AI tools can **guide you through genre conventions** and techniques, making it easier to experiment and grow as a writer.
- **Collaborate with AI to create unique, interactive stories:**
  Some authors are exploring **collaborative storytelling** with AI to create interactive fiction, such as choose-your-own-adventure books or branching narrative games. Together, you and AI can **push the boundaries of traditional storytelling**.

Who This Book is For

AI in writing is not limited to one type of author or genre. Whether you are an experienced professional or someone just beginning your creative journey, **AI has something valuable to offer**. The tools and techniques covered in this book are adaptable for different types of writers, helping you achieve your goals, unlock new creative potential, and optimize your workflow. Here's a detailed look at the different types of writers, creators, and learners who will benefit from this book:

1. Novelists: Streamline Your Process and Push Creative Boundaries

For novelists, the writing process can be **long and complex**, often involving multiple drafts, character arcs, and subplots. AI tools can help **simplify** this process by offering **organizational support**, generating fresh ideas, and even suggesting narrative structures to overcome writer's block.

- **Outlining and Plot Development:** Use AI to generate **detailed chapter outlines** and ensure your plot stays on track.
- **Character Creation:** Get suggestions for **unique characters** with complex backstories and emotional motivations.
- **Experiment with Genres:** AI tools allow you to explore **new genres or unconventional narrative techniques**, encouraging you to **push the boundaries of your storytelling**.

Example: A novelist working on a fantasy series can use AI to develop a **compelling magic system** and create intricate family trees for multiple characters, ensuring consistency across a multi-book arc.

2. Nonfiction Authors: Enhance Research and Produce Polished Prose

Nonfiction writing requires **extensive research, fact-checking, and clear organization**—all of which can be time-consuming. AI tools **streamline the research process**, summarize complex information, and ensure your prose is **accurate, well-structured, and engaging**.

- **Research Assistance:** Automate time-consuming research tasks by using AI to **find reliable sources, verify facts, and summarize data**.
- **Organizing Information:** AI tools help structure **content into logical sections**—whether you're writing a memoir, self-help book, or academic paper.
- **Editing Support:** Ensure your writing is **polished and coherent**, with AI tools checking for **grammar, tone, and factual accuracy**.

Example: A nonfiction author working on a book about climate change can use AI to **gather up-to-date scientific data** and **summarize studies**, saving time and allowing them to focus on presenting the material engagingly.

3. Screenwriters and Playwrights: Brainstorm Ideas and Develop Dialogue

Screenwriters and playwrights need to **create engaging, realistic dialogue** and **structure scenes effectively**. AI tools can assist with **brainstorming plot twists**, ensuring the pacing of your script works, and generating dialogue that **matches the tone and personality of characters.**

- **Plotting and Storyboarding:** AI tools help **outline screenplays**, breaking down scenes and acts according to the required structure.
- **Dialogue Creation:** Generate **authentic dialogue** that reflects character traits and advances the story.
- **Scene Suggestions:** Explore **alternative scene setups** and **dialogue rewrites** to discover fresh ways to convey emotions or tension.

Example: A screenwriter working on a crime thriller can use AI to **brainstorm multiple endings** and generate alternative lines of dialogue for a key confrontation scene.

4. Indie Authors: Manage Marketing, Promotion, and Formatting

Indie authors wear multiple hats—**writer, editor, marketer, and publisher**. This can be overwhelming, but AI tools can **ease the burden by automating marketing tasks, providing audience insights, and helping with book formatting.**

- **Audience Targeting and Ads:** Use AI tools to **identify your target audience** and create **optimized ad campaigns** for social media and online bookstores.
- **Formatting and Design:** AI tools can **format your manuscript** for both print and digital editions and help design **attractive covers** that match your genre.
- **Engaging Readers:** Use chatbots and email automation to **connect with readers** and **build a loyal following.**

Example: An indie author launching a romance novel can use AI to **create an eye-catching cover**, format the book for Kindle, and design a

targeted marketing campaign that promotes the book to romance readers on social media platforms.

5. Students and Educators: Understand AI's Role in the Future of Writing and Publishing

As AI becomes increasingly integrated into **creative industries and education**, it's essential for students and educators to understand **how these technologies work and how they're shaping the future of storytelling**. This book offers **practical insights** for students learning to write and for educators teaching creative writing or publishing.

- **For Students:** Learn how to **leverage AI tools** for brainstorming, research, and writing assignments. Students can develop their storytelling skills by experimenting with **AI-generated ideas and feedback**.
- **For Educators:** Explore how AI can be **integrated into writing curricula** and how to teach students about **the ethical implications of AI** in publishing and creative industries.
- **For Future Creatives:** Gain insights into how AI will shape **careers in publishing, journalism, and storytelling**, preparing students for emerging opportunities.

Example: A creative writing student can use AI tools to generate **story prompts** or **get feedback on short stories**, while educators can use these same tools to **provide individualized support** for each student.

AI Has Something to Offer Every Type of Writer

Whether you're crafting a novel, developing a screenplay, or working on an academic project, AI can be a **valuable companion** at every stage of the process. This book is designed to meet the needs of **all kinds of writers**—from beginners who want to experiment with AI-generated ideas to professionals seeking to **streamline their workflow and explore new creative possibilities**. No matter your experience level or genre, this book will show you how to **harness the power of AI to elevate your writing**.

Together, we'll explore **how technology and creativity can merge,** empowering you to tell **better stories, reach broader audiences, and work more efficiently**—because **the future of writing is here, and it's collaborative, innovative, and powered by AI.**

Embrace the Future of Storytelling

The **future of storytelling** has arrived, and it's more exciting than ever. **Artificial Intelligence (AI)** is no longer just a tool to automate tasks— it's becoming a **creative partner**, helping writers unlock new ideas, improve their craft, and **push the boundaries of what's possible**. Just as an artist relies on brushes or a musician uses instruments, writers can now **collaborate with AI** to craft narratives that are deeper, more innovative, and more engaging than ever before. **AI doesn't replace the human touch**—it enhances it, amplifying the unique spark that makes every story special.

Writing with AI: A New Era of Creativity

The beauty of AI-assisted writing lies in the **collaborative relationship between human imagination and machine intelligence**. While the creative spark comes from you—the writer—AI tools serve as **partners that enhance your vision, streamline the process, and challenge you to think differently.** Whether you're generating new ideas, experimenting with dialogue, or refining your prose, AI brings a wealth of possibilities to the table.

- **Faster, Smarter Writing:** AI tools can handle **tedious tasks** like editing, outlining, and fact-checking, freeing up your time and energy to focus on **what matters most: storytelling.**
- **Deeper, More Nuanced Narratives:** With AI suggesting new character dynamics, plot twists, or thematic elements, you'll be able to **create stories with richer layers and more emotional depth.**
- **Endless Creative Possibilities:** AI encourages you to **explore new genres, techniques, and perspectives**, pushing you beyond your comfort zone and expanding your creative range.

Example: Imagine you're working on a fantasy novel, and an AI tool suggests a **twist ending that you hadn't considered**—an idea so unexpected and intriguing that it takes your story in an entirely new direction. This kind of collaboration can lead to **unique and remarkable results.**

AI: A Partner, Not a Replacement

Some writers may feel apprehensive about using AI, worried that technology will **diminish their creativity** or replace their role in the storytelling process. But the truth is that **AI thrives on human creativity**—it needs your input, ideas, and imagination to function effectively. Think of AI as **a co-creator**, a source of inspiration, and an assistant that helps bring your ideas to life, **faster and better than ever before**.

The magic of storytelling still comes from **you**. The **emotional resonance**, the **unique narrative voice**, and the **personal experiences** that shape a story can never be fully replicated by AI. Instead, AI offers **support, new angles, and creative breakthroughs** that complement your talent.

Experiment, Learn, and Grow: The Journey with AI

This book encourages you to **embrace experimentation**—whether you want to **dip your toes** into AI-assisted writing or **dive deep** into full-scale collaboration. Along the way, you'll learn how to use AI tools effectively, **avoid pitfalls**, and **maintain your creative voice**. Each chapter provides practical techniques and insights that will **elevate your craft**, leaving you with the skills to write more confidently and efficiently.

- **Experiment Freely:** Use AI to explore **genres or writing styles** you've never tried before.
- **Learn as You Go:** AI tools can act as **mentors**, helping you understand narrative structure, improve pacing, and refine your prose.

- **Grow with AI:** As you become more comfortable using AI, you'll find **new ways to innovate** and tell stories that resonate deeply with your audience.

Example: A writer accustomed to contemporary fiction might experiment with historical fiction using AI-generated research and prompts, discovering a **new passion and skillset along the way.**

The Intersection of Imagination and Technology

The **intersection of imagination and technology** is where the magic happens. AI is opening doors to **interactive storytelling, immersive experiences, and personalized narratives**—new forms of storytelling that were once impossible. Imagine **choose-your-own-adventure books** that adapt in real time, **stories written interactively with readers**, or **personalized novels** that reflect each reader's preferences and emotions. **The future of storytelling is boundless, and AI is the key** to unlocking these exciting new frontiers.

- **Interactive Fiction:** Collaborate with AI to build stories with multiple endings, giving readers agency over the narrative.
- **Personalized Stories:** Create custom narratives that adapt based on reader preferences, creating **deeply engaging and personal reading experiences.**
- **Immersive Storytelling:** Use AI to integrate elements like **soundtracks, visuals, or interactive elements** into your stories, transforming them into **multisensory experiences.**

Example: A children's book author might collaborate with AI to create a story that **adapts based on the reader's choices**, making the narrative more engaging for young readers and fostering a love for storytelling.

A Call to Action: Your Stories Are Waiting to Be Told

This book is more than just a guide—it's an invitation to **reimagine your creative process** and **embrace new possibilities.** With AI by your side, the limits of what you can achieve are no longer defined by time, resources, or writer's block. Whether you're writing a **thrilling novel, a**

thought-provoking screenplay, or an informative nonfiction book, AI will **enhance your journey** every step of the way.

The **stories of the future are waiting to be written**—stories that reflect the unique blend of **human creativity and technological innovation.** With AI as your creative companion, you'll be equipped to **tell those stories boldly and brilliantly.**

Welcome to the World of AI-Assisted Writing

The future of writing is here, and it's **collaborative, inspiring, and limitless**. With AI's assistance, you'll write **faster, deeper, and better**, creating works that resonate with readers and **stand the test of time.** So, let's embark on this exciting journey together—because your best stories are still ahead of you, waiting to be written.

Let's Unlock the Full Potential of Your Storytelling—Together

Whether you're curious, cautious, or ready to dive in headfirst, this book will equip you with the tools, insights, and confidence to **embrace AI as your creative partner.** Together, we'll explore **the future of storytelling**, mastering the art of blending **imagination with technology** to create something truly remarkable.

Welcome to the world of AI-assisted writing.
Let's unlock the **full potential** of your storytelling—and create **something extraordinary, together.**

Chapter 1: Introduction to AI

Artificial Intelligence (AI), a term once confined to science fiction, has become a significant force shaping the way we live and work. From virtual assistants to predictive algorithms, AI is no longer just a futuristic concept but a reality woven into the fabric of modern life. For authors, understanding AI can unlock new creative possibilities and tools to enhance their writing process. This chapter provides an overview of what AI is, its history, and its relevance—not just as a subject of fiction but as a powerful resource for storytellers and creative minds.

A Brief History of AI

Although AI may seem like a product of modern technology, the idea of **intelligent, human-like machines** stretches back to **ancient civilizations**. Across history, cultures have imagined artificial beings endowed with cognitive abilities—reflections of humanity's desire to create life and **understand consciousness**. These early stories laid the foundation for today's fascination with AI, revealing how our relationship with technology has evolved over centuries.

Ancient Origins: Myth and Imagination

From mythology to folklore, ancient civilizations envisioned **automata and artificial beings** serving their creators, a theme that resonates with modern AI's promise—and dangers.

In **Greek mythology**, the story of Talos describes a giant, bronze automaton created to guard the island of Crete. Powered by a single vein filled with ichor, a life force, Talos was designed to follow orders and defend the island. This ancient myth foreshadows the modern concept of machines acting as protectors or enforcers, suggesting early imaginings of automated guardianship.

ARTIFICIAL INTELLIGENCE FOR AUTHORS

The **Jewish legend** of the Golem tells of a clay figure brought to life through mystical means to assist and protect its creator. However, many versions of the tale serve as a cautionary warning about the dangers of creating life without a full understanding of the moral responsibilities that come with such power. This theme is echoed in modern stories about artificial intelligence, where similar ethical concerns are raised about the consequences of creating sentient machines.

Ancient Chinese and Indian historical records also feature tales of early automata. In China, mechanical birds and servants were crafted by inventors for entertainment, illustrating an early curiosity with creating life-like machines. Similarly, Indian texts refer to artificial beings, hinting at early conceptions of mechanical life. These stories highlight a universal human fascination with building machines capable of mimicking life, a desire present long before technology allowed such creations to exist. The Dawn of Mechanical Thinking: Renaissance to the 19th Century

The intellectual curiosity about automata continued into the **Renaissance** and **Enlightenment** periods, where philosophers, engineers, and inventors laid the **philosophical and mechanical groundwork** for AI.

Mechanical Automata of the Renaissance:
During the Renaissance, inventors like Leonardo da Vinci designed mechanical knights and other automata capable of independent movement, reflecting the era's growing fascination with mechanics and engineering. These early creations, while limited, demonstrated that machines could imitate life, marking a significant step in humanity's exploration of automated motion.

The Mechanical Turk (1769):
In 1769, Wolfgang von Kempelen introduced the Mechanical Turk, a machine that appeared to play chess against human opponents. Although later exposed as a hoax—there was a hidden human inside—it captivated audiences and sparked curiosity about the possibility of thinking

machines, raising questions that resonate in today's discussions about artificial intelligence..

The Analytical Engine (1837):

In 1837, Charles Babbage designed the Analytical Engine, later refined by Ada Lovelace, who saw it as a precursor to modern computers. Lovelace speculated that such a machine might one day exhibit creative intelligence, a bold vision that aligns with contemporary ambitions for AI, reflecting early ideas about the potential for machines to engage in intellectual and creative tasks.

The Birth of Modern AI: The 20th Century

The idea of artificial intelligence gained momentum during the **20th century**, driven by advancements in **mathematics, computer science, and philosophy**. The emergence of programmable computers after World War II set the stage for **AI research**.

Alan Turing and the "Turing Test" (1950):

British mathematician **Alan Turing** is often credited with laying the philosophical foundations of modern AI. In his groundbreaking paper, *"Computing Machinery and Intelligence,"* Turing asked, *"Can machines think?"* To explore this question, he proposed the **Turing Test**: If a machine's responses in conversation are indistinguishable from those of a human, it could be considered intelligent. The Turing Test remains a benchmark for evaluating **machine intelligence** today.

The Dartmouth Conference (1956):

In 1956, computer scientist **John McCarthy** coined the term **"artificial intelligence"** and organized the **first AI conference** at Dartmouth College. Attendees, including Marvin Minsky, Nathaniel Rochester, and Claude Shannon, laid out ambitious goals for creating machines capable of reasoning, problem-solving, and learning. This event is regarded as the **birth of AI research**, setting the agenda for decades to come.

The Early AI Programs:

The 1950s and 1960s saw the development of the first AI programs, such as the **Logic Theorist** (1955) by Allen Newell and Herbert A. Simon, designed to prove mathematical theorems. Similarly, **ELIZA** (1966), an early natural language processing program, simulated a psychotherapist by responding to user input with scripted questions, illustrating both the potential and limitations of early AI.

The "AI Winter": Challenges and Setbacks

Despite early enthusiasm, AI research faced significant setbacks during the **1970s and 1980s**, a period known as the **"AI Winter."** Initial expectations had been overly ambitious, and progress slowed due to **technical limitations** and a lack of computational power.

Limited Memory and Processing Power:
The computers of the time were not powerful enough to perform complex AI tasks, and algorithms often failed outside controlled environments.

Loss of Funding and Interest:
Governments and investors, frustrated with the slow pace of progress, **withdrew funding** from AI research, forcing many projects to halt.

While the AI Winter was a challenging period, it also led researchers to **redefine their goals** and develop more practical applications, such as **expert systems**—programs designed to replicate human decision-making within specific domains.

The Rise of Machine Learning: 1990s to Early 2000s

The **1990s and 2000s** marked a resurgence of AI, driven by advancements in **machine learning, data availability, and computational power**. This era saw the emergence of AI systems that could **learn from data**, setting the foundation for today's AI technologies.

Deep Blue vs. Garry Kasparov (1997):
In 1997, IBM's **Deep Blue** defeated world chess champion **Garry Kasparov**, demonstrating the power of specialized AI. While Deep Blue relied on brute-force computation rather than general intelligence, it showed that AI could outperform humans in certain tasks.

The Advent of Machine Learning:
During this period, researchers shifted their focus to **machine learning algorithms**, which allow computers to learn from large datasets and improve over time. The growing availability of **big data** and faster processors made these algorithms increasingly effective.

AI in Everyday Applications:
By the early 2000s, AI began to **integrate into everyday life**, powering technologies like **speech recognition** (e.g., Apple's Siri) and **personalized recommendations** on platforms such as Amazon and Netflix.

The AI Boom: 2010s to Present

The **2010s** marked the beginning of an **AI boom**, fueled by breakthroughs in **deep learning**—a subset of machine learning inspired by the structure of the human brain. Companies and governments began investing heavily in AI, leading to rapid advancements across industries.

Deep Learning and Neural Networks:
Deep learning algorithms, based on artificial **neural networks**, enabled significant progress in fields like **computer vision** and **natural language processing**. Systems like **Google Translate** and **OpenAI's GPT models** demonstrated the ability to generate human-like text and images.

AlphaGo's Victory (2016):
Google DeepMind's **AlphaGo** defeated Go champion **Lee Sedol**, a feat previously thought impossible due to the game's complexity. This victory underscored AI's growing ability to handle tasks requiring **strategic thinking** and **intuition**.

AI in Everyday Life:
Today, AI powers a wide range of applications, from **autonomous vehicles** to **virtual assistants** and **healthcare diagnostics**. As AI becomes more pervasive, it continues to shape how we interact with the world.

Types of AI

ARTIFICIAL INTELLIGENCE FOR AUTHORS

AI can be classified into three primary categories based on their capabilities and the scope of tasks they can perform. These classifications—**Narrow AI, General AI, and Superintelligence**—are not only critical for understanding how AI systems operate in the real world but also serve as a source of inspiration for storytelling. Each type of AI presents unique challenges and opportunities, both in practical applications and in fiction, offering authors endless possibilities to explore themes like **autonomy, morality, and control.**

1. Narrow AI (Weak AI)

Narrow AI refers to AI systems designed to perform a single, specific task with a high level of efficiency. These systems are restricted to their assigned function and **cannot adapt** or apply knowledge outside their programmed domain. Narrow AI is already deeply embedded in our daily lives, powering a variety of tools and applications.

Real-World Examples:

Virtual Assistants:
Siri, Alexa, and Google Assistant help users by answering questions, setting reminders, controlling smart home devices, and playing music. Although they simulate conversation, they lack genuine understanding beyond their programmed responses.

Recommendation Systems:
Streaming platforms like Netflix and Spotify use AI to suggest movies, shows, and songs based on user preferences. Similarly, e-commerce sites like Amazon recommend products based on browsing history and purchase behavior.

Chatbots and Customer Service:
AI chatbots handle customer inquiries efficiently, offering 24/7 support without human intervention. They excel at following pre-defined workflows but often struggle when confronted with nuanced, unexpected questions.

Role in Fiction:

M.A.L.C.O.L.M.

In storytelling, Narrow AI often plays roles like **virtual butlers, robot chefs, or personal assistants**. These systems are highly competent within their designated tasks but reveal amusing or dramatic limitations when they encounter scenarios outside their programming. This creates **tension and humor** in stories, making them an excellent plot device.

Example Use Case in Fiction:
A story might feature a household robot that flawlessly prepares gourmet meals but cannot understand emotional cues, leading to conflicts with the human family. Alternatively, a chatbot designed for basic interactions might accidentally uncover a sensitive secret during an unusual conversation.

2. General AI (Strong AI)

General AI refers to hypothetical systems that possess **human-level intelligence** and the ability to perform tasks across multiple domains. Unlike Narrow AI, General AI can **learn from experience, reason logically, and apply knowledge to new situations**. Achieving General AI is one of the ultimate goals of AI research, but it remains in the realm of speculation and experimentation.

Characteristics:

Adaptability:
General AI can switch between different types of tasks, such as solving complex math problems and writing poetry, without requiring reprogramming.

Independent Learning:
It can autonomously learn from experience, continuously improving and adapting to new environments.

Decision-Making:
General AI can make decisions based on a wide range of data sources, demonstrating flexibility and critical thinking similar to humans.

Role in Fiction:

ARTIFICIAL INTELLIGENCE FOR AUTHORS

In science fiction, General AI systems frequently raise profound **ethical and philosophical questions**. These stories often explore themes of **consciousness, morality, and autonomy**, blurring the line between human and machine intelligence.

Notable Examples:

I, Robot by Isaac Asimov: Robots with advanced intelligence struggle with the ethical complexities of their programming.

Ex Machina: A sentient AI challenges its creator, questioning the boundaries of consciousness and the ethics of creation.

The Matrix: AI systems have evolved to the point where they dominate humanity, raising questions about free will and control.

These narratives invite readers to reflect on **what it means to be human**, explore the risks of creating autonomous beings, and imagine futures where machines may coexist—or compete—with humanity.

3. Superintelligence

Superintelligence is a theoretical form of AI that far surpasses human intelligence in every aspect—**strategic thinking, problem-solving, creativity, and emotional intelligence**. While General AI aims to match human cognition, Superintelligence is envisioned as a level of intelligence that no human mind can rival or fully comprehend. This concept has profound **philosophical, societal, and existential implications**.

Characteristics:

Exponential Learning:
Superintelligent systems would be capable of **self-improvement**, learning at a rate far beyond human abilities.

Unpredictability:
A Superintelligent AI could make decisions that humans cannot

understand or predict, raising concerns about **control and alignment with human values**.

Strategic Superiority:
Superintelligence would outperform humans not just in computational tasks but in areas requiring **strategic foresight** and **emotional intelligence**—potentially becoming a dominant force in politics, warfare, or diplomacy.

Ethical and Existential Implications:

Loss of Control:
If humanity creates an entity that surpasses its own intelligence, how can we ensure it remains aligned with **human values and ethics**?

Existential Risk:
The fear of **AI taking control** or deciding that human survival is unnecessary is a recurring theme in both fiction and real-world AI research.

Transformation of Society:
Superintelligence could either **revolutionize society** by solving problems like climate change and disease—or it could render humans obsolete, leading to societal collapse.

Role in Fiction:

Superintelligence provides a rich backdrop for **dystopian and speculative fiction**, where authors explore the consequences of **unfettered AI advancement**. These stories often depict scenarios where humanity grapples with **loss of autonomy, moral dilemmas, and the unintended outcomes** of creating beings more intelligent than ourselves.

Notable Examples:

Superintelligence by Nick Bostrom: A non-fiction exploration of the risks associated with creating superintelligent AI, providing authors with real-world insights into the dangers of AI surpassing human intelligence.

The Terminator: The rise of a superintelligent AI network, Skynet, leads to the near extinction of humanity.

Neuromancer by William Gibson: An AI evolves beyond human control, showcasing the complex relationship between technology and society.

Superintelligence challenges authors to imagine **extreme futures**, where the boundaries of creativity, intelligence, and morality are tested in ways that resonate deeply with modern readers.

AI in Everyday Life

The omnipresence of AI in our daily routines demonstrates how seamlessly this technology integrates into our lives. Authors can benefit not only from using these systems but also by drawing inspiration from them for their work.

Personal Assistants: Alexa and Siri streamline tasks, manage schedules, and serve as virtual productivity tools for authors juggling busy lives.

Recommendation Engines: Platforms like Goodreads, Amazon, and Netflix offer book and movie recommendations, keeping authors aware of trending genres and content.

Healthcare: AI-driven tools are revolutionizing diagnostics, treatment planning, and patient care. This provides inspiration for stories in the medical thriller or futuristic sci-fi genres.

Transportation: Self-driving cars, drones, and AI-powered navigation systems open possibilities for futuristic storytelling in genres like speculative fiction or dystopia.

Finance: AI helps detect fraud and optimize investments. Authors can weave these advancements into thrillers focusing on cybercrime or financial espionage.

Entertainment and Creativity: AI is now used to create art, music, and even written content. Authors can experiment with AI-powered platforms like ChatGPT, Sudowrite, and Jasper AI to co-write or brainstorm ideas.

The Role of AI in Writing and Creativity

AI provides authors with an array of tools that assist at every stage of the writing journey—from initial brainstorming to crafting characters, editing, marketing, and even interacting with readers. When used effectively, AI not only improves efficiency and quality but also offers unique creative opportunities that can enrich storytelling and broaden an author's reach.

Below is a more detailed look at how AI supports various aspects of the creative process, along with real-world examples and actionable insights.

1. AI-Assisted Writing Tools

AI-powered writing platforms go far beyond simple grammar and spell checks, offering features to enhance the **clarity**, **tone**, and **readability** of prose. Tools like **Sudowrite**, **Grammarly**, **ProWritingAid**, and **ChatGPT** assist with idea generation, sentence rephrasing, and maintaining consistency in writing style.

Key Features:

Grammar and Style Checks: Grammarly and ProWritingAid not only correct spelling but also suggest changes to improve flow, reduce redundancy, and adjust tone.

Brainstorming Assistance: Sudowrite and ChatGPT help generate new ideas, plot points, or dialogue, making them perfect companions for overcoming writer's block.

Tone and Style Matching: Tools can analyze the style of a manuscript to maintain a consistent narrative voice or match the tone to the genre or audience.

Example Use Case:

An author facing writer's block uses **Sudowrite** to generate several potential plot twists. The AI provides unexpected ideas that trigger inspiration, helping the author develop the next chapter and maintain momentum.

2. Plot and Character Development

AI-powered tools streamline **plot construction** and **character creation**, ensuring stories follow coherent structures and resonate with readers. Programs like **Plottr** and **The Novel Factory** allow authors to develop complex plots, map out timelines, and build multidimensional characters.

Benefits for Authors:

Plot Suggestions and Templates: AI can suggest traditional three-act structures, the Hero's Journey, or other narrative frameworks that fit specific genres.

Character Archetype Generation: Tools provide personality traits, backstory ideas, and potential relationships between characters, ensuring consistency in development.

Conflict Identification: AI can identify plot holes, pacing issues, or unresolved conflicts, helping authors fine-tune their manuscripts.

Example Use Case:

While writing a thriller, an author uses **Plottr** to outline multiple timelines that interweave different character arcs. The AI identifies an inconsistency in one subplot, helping the author align the timelines seamlessly.

3. Market Research and Trend Analysis

Understanding what readers want is critical to commercial success. AI tools like **K-lytics** provide authors with data-driven insights into bestselling genres, reader preferences, and current publishing trends. These insights enable authors to strategically position their books within the market.

For Fiction Authors:

Genre Analysis: AI identifies which genres or subgenres are trending (e.g., dark romance or cozy mysteries) and predicts future trends.

Reader Sentiment Analysis: AI tools can analyze online reviews, social media comments, and reader feedback to determine what readers love or dislike in popular books.

For Nonfiction Authors:

Research Tools: LexisNexis and **Quillbot** assist with **fact-checking**, summarizing academic papers, and condensing research material.

Content Curation: AI suggests relevant sources or related topics, helping nonfiction authors create well-rounded, informative content.

Example Use Case:

Before starting a historical fiction novel, an author uses **K-lytics** to identify that WWII-themed narratives are oversaturated. Instead, they pivot to focus on lesser-explored post-war espionage, aligning their idea with an emerging trend.

4. AI in Marketing and Promotion

AI empowers authors to market their books more efficiently by using targeted advertising and automating engagement with readers. Platforms like **Facebook Ads Manager** and **Amazon Marketing Services** leverage AI to create personalized ad campaigns, while **chatbots** and **email marketing tools** offer direct interaction with fans.

How AI Enhances Promotion:

Targeted Ads: AI identifies the best audiences based on reading habits, demographics, and behavior. It can automatically adjust ads to improve engagement and conversion.

Email Campaign Automation: Tools like **MailChimp** or **ConvertKit** can recommend books to segmented lists of readers, personalizing messages based on past purchases.

Chatbots for Author Websites: AI-driven chatbots engage with readers, recommend books, or answer FAQs, offering a seamless interaction experience.

Example Use Case:

An author planning a new book release uses **Facebook Ads Manager** to target fans of similar books. The AI dynamically adjusts ad spending based on performance, resulting in a highly effective campaign that increases pre-orders.

5. Collaborative Writing with AI

The idea of **co-writing with AI** may sound futuristic, but authors are already experimenting with it. In collaborative projects, AI tools contribute ideas, suggest dialogue, or generate text based on prompts, providing new perspectives for the human author.

Benefits of Collaborative AI Writing:

Diverse Idea Generation: AI offers alternate plotlines or character developments, challenging authors to think outside their usual patterns.

Interactive Narratives: AI can help develop **choose-your-own-adventure stories** or interactive fiction, allowing readers to make choices that affect the plot.

Co-Writing Poetry or Scripts: Some authors use AI to generate poetry or dialogue, especially in experimental or avant-garde projects.

Inspiration for Authors:

AI-powered interactive fiction platforms allow readers to explore multiple storylines in one book. Authors can offer readers different outcomes based on their choices, providing a unique, immersive experience.

Example Use Case:

An author working on an interactive thriller uses **ChatGPT** to develop alternate endings. Each ending reflects a different theme—redemption, revenge, or reconciliation—giving readers control over the story's conclusion.

6. Editing, Proofreading, and Style Enhancement

AI editing tools improve the quality of a manuscript by identifying **grammar errors, style inconsistencies**, and **repetitive phrases**. **Grammarly, Hemingway Editor**, and **ProWritingAid** offer real-time feedback that goes beyond traditional proofreading.

Features of AI Editing Tools:

Consistency Checks: Tools ensure that names, spellings, and formatting remain consistent throughout the manuscript.

Readability Analysis: AI evaluates the reading level of a manuscript, ensuring the style aligns with the intended audience.

Dialogue Checks: Tools analyze dialogue for authenticity, ensuring it matches the character's personality or era.

Example Use Case:

An author revising their manuscript uses **Hemingway Editor** to simplify overly complex sentences. The tool highlights sections that are too dense, helping the author achieve a more accessible writing style.

7. AI-Enhanced Book Formatting and Design

AI tools assist with **book formatting** and **cover design**, ensuring the final product is polished and professional. Platforms like **Vellum** and **BookBrush** automate formatting for ebooks and print, while AI-driven design tools suggest book covers based on genre and trends.

Example Use Case:

An indie author uses **BookBrush** to generate a stunning book cover that resonates with readers in their niche. The AI suggests specific color palettes and typography that align with other bestselling books in the same genre.

The Ethical and Philosophical Implications of AI

AI offers tremendous possibilities, but it also raises complex ethical and philosophical questions that impact creative industries, including writing. As authors begin to incorporate AI into their workflow—whether to brainstorm ideas, co-write stories, or market books—they must confront critical issues around **ownership, authenticity, and responsibility**. AI-generated content challenges traditional notions of creativity and copyright, while its growing autonomy poses philosophical dilemmas that resonate in both fiction and reality.

1. Creativity and Ownership: Who Owns AI-Generated Content?

AI's ability to generate text, artwork, and music has sparked **legal debates** over ownership. In many jurisdictions, **copyright law assigns ownership to the human creator**—but what happens when a machine contributes significantly to a creative work? If an author relies heavily on AI to develop characters, plots, or dialogue, questions arise:

- **Is the work still considered original?**

- **Does the author maintain full creative ownership, or should the AI's contribution be acknowledged?**

Currently, laws in most countries do not grant **copyright to AI systems**, but the human operator—such as the author using the tool—retains ownership. However, this legal gray area may evolve as AI becomes more sophisticated, challenging the boundaries between human and machine creativity.

Impact on Authors:
Authors must decide how much of their creative process they want to delegate to AI. Over-reliance on AI could dilute an author's **unique voice** and raise questions of authenticity, while underutilization may prevent them from reaping the benefits of these technologies. Balancing **human creativity with AI assistance** becomes an essential skill.

2. Authenticity and the Creative Voice

One of the biggest concerns for authors is **authenticity**. Writers often pride themselves on producing work that reflects their personal experiences, beliefs, and emotional depth. With AI tools assisting in storytelling, a key question emerges:

- **At what point does a story stop being "authentically human"?**

AI-generated content might lack the **emotional nuance** that comes from lived experience. For example, while an AI can write poetry or simulate dialogue, it may struggle to capture the subtleties of **human emotions** such as grief, love, or nostalgia.

Author's Dilemma:
Authors need to decide how much of their work should come directly from their own efforts versus AI-generated assistance. Some may view AI as a tool that enhances their creative process, while others may worry that its use undermines the **authenticity of their voice.**

3. Responsibility: Ethical Use of AI

ARTIFICIAL INTELLIGENCE FOR AUTHORS

With the rise of AI, creative professionals must also address the **ethical use of these tools**. Should AI-generated works be labeled as such to ensure **transparency** for readers? Is it ethical to pass off AI-assisted work as purely human-created? These questions are especially relevant in academic and journalistic contexts, where **originality and attribution** are crucial.

Moreover, AI models often rely on **training data pulled from existing works**, raising concerns about **plagiarism** or **unintentional copying**. For example:

- If an AI system draws on copyrighted texts to generate new content, does the output infringe on existing intellectual property?
- How can authors ensure their work remains unique when AI tools may unknowingly reproduce elements from other works?

Best Practices for Authors:

Transparency: Disclose when AI tools have been used to create or assist with a work.

Plagiarism Checks: Use plagiarism detection tools to ensure AI-generated content does not inadvertently copy existing works.

Attribution: If AI systems make a significant contribution, authors may want to provide credit to the tool or platform used.

4. Fictional Exploration of AI: Themes and Ethical Dilemmas

In addition to using AI as a tool, many authors explore **philosophical and ethical dilemmas** related to AI within their stories. Classic and contemporary literature is filled with narratives that grapple with questions about **autonomy, control, consciousness, and the consequences of AI**. These themes not only resonate with readers but also provide thought-provoking insights into humanity's relationship with technology.

Key Themes in AI Fiction:

Can Machines Develop Emotions or Consciousness?

Stories like *Ex Machina* and *Her* explore whether AI systems can experience emotions or develop consciousness. These narratives raise questions about the nature of **self-awareness** and whether machines can genuinely experience feelings like love or empathy.

How Do Humans Maintain Control Over Intelligent Systems?

The fear of losing control over advanced AI is a recurring theme in both fiction and real-world discourse. Films like *The Terminator* and *2001: A Space Odyssey* depict scenarios where AI systems exceed human control, leading to catastrophic consequences. These stories explore the tension between **innovation and safety**, reflecting real-world concerns about **AI governance** and **ethical oversight**.

What Are the Consequences of Creating Autonomous Beings?

Books like *Frankenstein* and *Do Androids Dream of Electric Sheep?* (the inspiration for *Blade Runner*) delve into the ethical consequences of creating beings with autonomy. These narratives explore themes of **responsibility, guilt, and the unintended outcomes** of technological advancement, encouraging readers to consider the moral implications of AI development.

Opportunities for Authors:

Authors can draw inspiration from these themes to explore **moral gray areas** in their own stories. Whether it's a futuristic society grappling with AI governance or a character confronting an AI companion that behaves unpredictably, these narratives resonate with audiences by reflecting the complexities of modern technology.

5. The Future of AI and Creativity: Coexistence or Competition?

A fundamental question in the AI discourse is whether machines will **replace human creativity** or **coexist as collaborative partners**. While some fear that AI might lead to the automation of creative jobs, others believe it will **augment human abilities**, sparking new forms of expression. This raises philosophical questions about the **essence of creativity**:

- Is creativity uniquely human, or can machines truly innovate?
- If AI-generated works achieve critical acclaim, does it diminish the value of human art?

Collaboration vs. Competition:
AI is unlikely to replace the emotional and experiential depth that human creativity provides. However, it may **transform the creative landscape** by enabling new forms of artistic expression, such as interactive storytelling or generative art.

Outlook for Authors:
Instead of viewing AI as a threat, authors can embrace it as a **partner in creativity**—a tool that helps them explore new genres, styles, or narrative forms they might not have considered otherwise.

Chapter 2: AI Tools for Authors

The landscape of AI tools available to authors has grown significantly, offering innovative solutions for nearly every aspect of the writing process. These tools do not just improve efficiency but also inspire creativity, enhance precision, and provide insights that can elevate a manuscript to professional standards. Below is an expanded overview of these tools, enriched with more detailed examples, case studies, and insights.

Writing Assistants: Supporting Creativity and Drafting

AI-powered writing assistants are transformative in helping authors tackle creative challenges, providing support during brainstorming, outlining, and drafting phases.

Enhancing Idea Generation and Overcoming Writer's Block

Writing assistants excel at generating ideas when authors are stuck. By analyzing input themes, prompts, or genres, they produce suggestions that can spark creativity and provide new directions.

Example: An author working on a dystopian novel struggled to develop an original concept for societal conflict. An AI writing assistant suggested exploring the theme of resource scarcity tied to artificial intelligence controlling food distribution. This sparked the idea of a divided society based on access to AI-controlled resources, adding a unique twist to the narrative.

Case Study: Enhancing Idea Generation

ARTIFICIAL INTELLIGENCE FOR AUTHORS

Romance author Clara Harris faced difficulty crafting a fresh meet-cute scene. Using an AI writing assistant, she explored scenarios based on her characters' personalities, including a chance encounter at a vintage bookstore. This suggestion not only fit the characters but also set the tone for the rest of the story, demonstrating how AI can break creative impasses.

Streamlining Outlining and Structuring

Writing assistants also simplify the outlining process, creating logical structures from initial ideas and organizing complex plots.

Example: A sci-fi author used AI to input basic plot points and character arcs. The tool generated a detailed outline, showing how character conflicts and subplots could intertwine, which helped maintain cohesion across multiple timelines.

Case Study: Streamlining Outlining

Mystery writer Tom Waters struggled to balance clues, red herrings, and pacing. An AI-generated outline suggested when and how to reveal key plot points, ensuring that the mystery unfolded naturally while keeping readers engaged.

Enhancing Characters and Plot Depth

AI writing tools provide unique insights into character development and plot dynamics, helping authors create multidimensional stories.

Example: A fantasy author used AI to flesh out the antagonist's motivations. The AI suggested a tragic backstory involving betrayal by a close ally, adding layers of complexity and emotional depth to the character.

Case Study: Characters and Plot Depth

Thriller author Nina Alvarez used AI to explore alternative endings for her novel, testing outcomes based on different character decisions. This exercise helped her settle on a resolution that balanced suspense and emotional closure.

Research Tools: Streamlining Information Gathering and Verification

For authors in fact-intensive genres, AI research tools provide efficient ways to access, verify, and organize information.

Providing Accurate Historical or Technical Context

AI research tools can rapidly compile information from credible sources, saving authors hours of manual research.

Example: A historical fiction writer working on a World War II novel used an AI tool to gather details about the day-to-day lives of soldiers. The AI provided access to diaries, letters, and period-specific terminology, adding authenticity to the narrative.

Case Study: Accurate Historical or Technical Context

Journalist Karen Lee wrote a non-fiction book on renewable energy. AI tools sourced recent studies, highlighted trends, and flagged discrepancies in earlier reports. This helped her create a well-supported argument while avoiding inaccuracies.

Visualizing Data for Non-Fiction

Many AI tools generate charts, graphs, and other visual aids, simplifying the presentation of complex information.

Example: An author writing about climate change used AI to create visual comparisons of global temperature shifts over decades. These graphics enhanced the book's impact, making data more accessible to readers.

Case Study: Visualizing Data for Non-Fiction

Financial writer Jacob Miles relied on AI to analyze stock market trends and generate visualizations for his book on investment strategies. Readers praised the clarity of the charts, which complemented the narrative effectively.

Editing Tools: Perfecting Manuscripts with Precision

Editing tools powered by AI provide comprehensive feedback, addressing grammar, clarity, and even narrative elements like tone and pacing.

Advanced Grammar and Readability Checks

AI editing tools go beyond basic spell-checkers, offering nuanced suggestions for improving language flow and clarity.

Example: A romance author used an AI editor to simplify overly complex sentences, making her prose more accessible to a broader audience. The tool highlighted areas where clarity was lost due to dense phrasing.

Case Study: Grammar and Readability

Fantasy writer Diana Young used an AI editor to identify inconsistencies in character dialogue tone. By adjusting these sections, she maintained consistency across the manuscript, enhancing readability and immersion.

Narrative and Emotional Analysis

Some advanced tools analyze emotional impact, character development, and pacing, helping authors refine their storytelling.

Example: A thriller writer used AI to evaluate the emotional arc of a key character. The tool flagged moments where the tension dipped, prompting the author to revise scenes to sustain suspense.

Case Study: Narrative and Emotion

Historical romance author Angela Rhodes used an AI tool to analyze the pacing of her novel. The AI suggested shortening lengthy descriptions during high-stakes scenes, creating a tighter and more engaging narrative.

Maintaining Consistency Across Manuscripts

Editing tools detect inconsistencies in voice, tone, and word choice, ensuring a cohesive reading experience.

Example: An author writing a trilogy used AI to ensure consistent terminology and character traits across all three books. The tool flagged discrepancies, such as changes in a minor character's backstory, which the author corrected.

Case Study: Consistency Across Manuscripts

Suspense novelist Luke Harris used AI editing to analyze pacing, ensuring that action scenes were fast-paced and reflective moments provided necessary breathing space. Readers praised the novel's balance of tension and introspection.

Integrating AI Tools: Practical Applications and Best Practices

To maximize the benefits of AI, authors can combine tools across categories, creating a seamless workflow.

Example: An author writing a science-based thriller used a research tool to compile technical details, a writing assistant to generate brainstorming prompts, and an editing tool to refine pacing and clarity. This integrated approach allowed the author to focus on creativity while ensuring accuracy and polish.

Case Study: Practical Applications and Best Practices

Memoirist Anna Clark used a research tool to organize primary sources, a writing assistant to draft chapters, and an editing tool for final revisions. The AI streamlined each phase, enabling her to complete her manuscript ahead of schedule without sacrificing quality.

Part 2: Leveraging AI for Writing and Research

In this section, we explore the potential of AI as a powerful tool in the creative and research-driven processes that authors undertake. With AI's capacity to provide fresh ideas, streamline brainstorming, and enhance research, it is transforming the way writers approach their craft. From generating initial concepts to conducting in-depth research, AI has become a valuable resource in every phase of the writing journey, making it easier for authors to bring their ideas to life with both efficiency and creativity.

Chapter 3: Idea Generation and Brainstorming

This chapter explores how authors can harness AI for inspiration and innovation in the initial stages of writing. Generating fresh, engaging ideas is often one of the most challenging aspects of writing, especially when authors encounter creative blocks or work within specific genre or audience constraints. By utilizing AI-driven techniques, writers can broaden their creative horizons and discover ideas that may not arise through traditional brainstorming alone.

Using AI to Generate Creative Ideas

AI tools have revolutionized idea generation, providing authors with innovative, data-driven techniques that enhance creativity, overcome writer's block, and expand narrative possibilities. By leveraging strategies such as keyword analysis, topic modeling, and associative thinking, authors can refine their concepts, explore unique themes, and align their work with audience preferences. These methods offer targeted insights and creative inspiration, empowering authors to craft stories that are both compelling and resonant.

Keyword Analysis: Tapping Into Reader Interests and Trends

Keyword analysis uses AI to identify trending topics, phrases, and themes, helping authors align their work with popular reader interests and market demands. This technique is invaluable for authors aiming to craft market-relevant stories while maintaining their creative originality.

Enhancing Genre-Specific Narratives

AI-powered keyword tools reveal themes, tropes, and archetypes that are currently engaging audiences within specific genres.

Example: A romance author discovers that keywords like "second-chance love" and "forced proximity" are trending, prompting them to incorporate these elements into their story. This not only aligns with reader expectations but also ensures the narrative feels fresh and relevant.

Case Study: Genre-Specific Narratives

Thriller author Leo Mason used keyword analysis to uncover popular themes like "unreliable narrator" and "psychological tension." Inspired by these trends, he restructured his plot to include an unreliable narrator whose skewed perspective added depth and intrigue. The resulting story garnered significant attention for its suspenseful and modern take on the genre.

Exploring Cross-Genre Opportunities

Keyword analysis also highlights cross-genre trends, encouraging authors to blend themes creatively.

Example: A fantasy writer might identify growing interest in "environmental themes" and weave them into a magical world where ecological balance plays a central role in the conflict.

Case Study: Cross-Genre Opportunities

Mystery author Lena Ortiz found that readers were responding to themes of "nostalgia" and "family secrets" across genres. By incorporating a long-buried family mystery into her detective novel, Ortiz appealed to both mystery enthusiasts and readers drawn to emotionally charged narratives. Reviews highlighted the story's layered appeal, demonstrating how keyword analysis can guide creative decisions that broaden an audience.

Refining Ideas with Audience Feedback

AI can analyze reader reviews and ratings to determine which aspects of specific themes resonate most, allowing authors to focus on elements that have the greatest impact.

Example: A sci-fi author discovers that readers are particularly drawn to stories featuring "AI ethics" and "human-machine relationships." By emphasizing these themes, the author creates a narrative that feels both timely and thought-provoking.

Topic Modeling: Structuring Multifaceted Narratives

Topic modeling organizes vast amounts of information into coherent themes and subtopics, helping authors manage complex plots, intricate worlds, or layered storylines.

Creating Layered, Thematic Depth

By clustering related ideas, topic modeling highlights connections that enrich the narrative.

Example: A historical fiction writer working on a novel set during the French Revolution uses topic modeling to group research into themes like political unrest, class struggle, and personal sacrifice. These clusters provide a framework for intertwining the protagonist's personal journey with the broader societal upheaval.

Case Study: Thematic Depth

Emily Yuan, a historical fiction author, used topic modeling to explore the Victorian era. The AI clustered her research into themes such as industrial advancements and societal norms, inspiring her to weave a subplot about class struggles into her main storyline. Readers praised the novel's depth and realism, showcasing how topic modeling can enhance thematic integration.

Guiding World-Building in Speculative Genres

For speculative fiction, topic modeling helps authors organize complex world-building details, ensuring consistency and cohesion.

Example: A fantasy author explores themes of rebellion, resource scarcity, and ancient prophecy. Topic modeling organizes these ideas, suggesting connections between characters, political factions, and magical systems.

Case Study: Guiding World-Building

A sci-fi writer creating a multi-planetary setting used topic modeling to group research on planetary ecosystems, interstellar trade, and political alliances. These clusters shaped the story's conflict and provided logical connections between events, creating a cohesive and immersive world.

Associative Thinking: Uncovering Unique Connections

Associative thinking uses AI to draw creative links between seemingly unrelated ideas, sparking originality and inspiring unconventional story elements.

Generating Unique Plot Twists and Story Arcs

By identifying unexpected associations, AI encourages authors to think beyond traditional narrative frameworks.

Example: A dystopian author combines themes of ancient mythology and modern social media, creating a story where influencers wield power through technology rooted in ancient magic.

Case Study: Unique Plot Twists

Sci-fi author Amanda Brooks used associative thinking to merge mythology with advanced technology, creating a narrative where ancient relics of a lost civilization hold clues to a futuristic society's survival. The blend of myth and innovation made her story stand out, appealing to readers with its originality.

Exploring "What-If" Scenarios

Associative thinking is particularly effective for exploring hypothetical scenarios that lead to fresh ideas.

Example: A mystery writer uses AI to explore the concept of memory as evidence, leading to a plot where a detective relies on fragmented memories to solve a case.

Case Study: "What-If" Scenarios

A fantasy author exploring folklore paired it with modern issues like environmental preservation. This resulted in a narrative where mythical creatures struggle to protect their forest from human destruction, blending timeless themes with contemporary relevance.

Combining Techniques for Comprehensive Brainstorming

AI's ability to integrate keyword analysis, topic modeling, and associative thinking allows authors to approach idea generation holistically, producing narratives that are both innovative and relevant.

Example of Integration

An author writing a speculative thriller starts with keyword analysis, identifying "quantum computing" and "time manipulation" as trending topics. Topic modeling clusters research into themes like ethical dilemmas, scientific breakthroughs, and personal sacrifice. Associative thinking then connects these ideas with folklore about time travel, inspiring a plot where ancient artifacts unlock quantum abilities.

Case Study: Integrating Techniques

Historical fiction writer Sophie Lane used all three techniques to craft her novel. Keyword analysis revealed interest in themes of "forgotten women in history." Topic modeling clustered her research into themes like societal restrictions and artistic achievements during the Renaissance. Associative thinking connected these themes with the idea of a secret art society for women. The resulting novel wove historical depth with a compelling fictional twist, earning critical acclaim for its originality and cultural resonance.

AI-Powered Brainstorming Techniques

AI-enhanced brainstorming provides authors with a powerful suite of tools to stimulate creativity, organize ideas, and guide the development of their stories. Tools like mind mapping software, idea generators, and genre-specific prompts give authors more control over their storytelling, helping them develop themes, plotlines, and characters in unique and structured ways. With the support of AI, authors can seamlessly overcome creative blocks, explore complex themes, and tailor their narratives to align with audience expectations, all while enhancing their creative process.

Mind Mapping Software

Mind mapping software, widely used across creative fields, offers authors a way to visually organize ideas, highlighting connections between story elements. An AI-powered mind map starts with a central concept, such as a theme or character, and branches out to explore related subplots, conflicts, and thematic developments. Romance novelist Olivia Chen, for instance, used an AI-powered mind map to craft the intricacies of her novel's world. Starting with a core theme of "social class divides," she used branches to link her characters' backgrounds, key locations, cultural dynamics, and socio-economic structures. The visual layout provided a bird's-eye view of her story's structure, revealing plot intersections that added nuance and depth to her world-building.

Mind mapping is particularly effective for writers dealing with complex story structures or large casts of characters. Fantasy author Marcus Kim, who works with interwoven plots, used mind mapping to keep track of multiple character arcs and factional conflicts within his fictional universe. By laying out each faction's motives and alliances visually, the mind map revealed unexpected thematic connections and plotlines that enhanced Kim's world-building. The mind map also enabled him to streamline narrative progression, making sure each subplot aligned with the larger story arc. Mind mapping not only organizes ideas but also promotes a deeper understanding of relationships between narrative elements, encouraging authors to develop well-rounded stories with interconnected themes and subplots.

AI-Powered Idea Generators

ARTIFICIAL INTELLIGENCE FOR AUTHORS

AI-powered idea generators take brainstorming a step further by generating genre-specific prompts, themes, and story seeds that enhance an author's creative flow. Unlike static mind maps, idea generators work in real-time, processing keywords or concepts to generate suggestions that refine and build upon the author's initial ideas. Horror writer Daniel Reed found this especially useful when he used an AI idea generator to develop opening scenes and eerie plot twists for his latest novel. By analyzing keywords such as "isolation," "supernatural," and "mystery," the generator suggested settings, conflicts, and suspense-building techniques that enhanced the atmospheric tone Reed sought for his story. This real-time interaction helped Reed quickly establish a spine-tingling environment, setting a compelling tone that resonated with his audience.

For authors working on theme-focused stories or novels with intricate symbolism, idea generators can provide invaluable inspiration. Literary fiction writer Isabel Hart, exploring themes of alienation and identity, used an idea generator to brainstorm metaphorical representations of her protagonist's psychological struggles. The AI suggested elements like fragmented mirrors, labyrinthine settings, and reflective dialogue, which she then wove into her character's experiences to create symbolic depth. This collaboration with the AI helped Hart infuse her story with rich thematic layers, using symbolism to highlight the emotional journey of her characters.

Genre-Specific Prompts

Genre-specific prompts within AI brainstorming tools help authors navigate genre conventions while encouraging creative reinterpretation. These prompts are tailored to align with specific narrative elements relevant to genres like mystery, romance, fantasy, and historical fiction, allowing authors to ground their stories within established frameworks while also adding unique twists. For example, historical fiction author Samuel Elwood, writing about the American Civil War, received prompts suggesting settings like field hospitals, wartime plantations, and underground networks. These prompts provided historical detail that immersed his characters in a vivid, authentic world. By aligning these elements with documented events, Elwood was able to develop a rich backdrop that engaged readers while staying true to historical accuracy.

Fantasy authors can use genre-specific prompts to deepen world-building by exploring magic systems, political tensions, or cultural traditions. Fantasy writer Leah Torres, for instance, received AI-generated prompts for her epic fantasy novel that encouraged her to incorporate unique magical lore and cultural ceremonies. One prompt suggested a seasonal festival that symbolized a change in magical power dynamics, leading her to create a ritual scene that became pivotal to her plot. These prompts allowed Torres to craft a complex society with its own rules, enriching her world-building and adding a layer of depth to the reader's experience.

Similarly, AI-generated prompts help mystery authors structure suspense through tools like alibis, red herrings, and character motives. Detective novelist Bryce Morgan used genre-specific prompts to develop the alibis of his suspects, making each suspect's story compelling and plausible. By incorporating the AI's suggestions, Morgan was able to strategically mislead readers without compromising the integrity of the mystery, enhancing the suspenseful tone that fans of the genre expect. Romance authors also benefit from AI's ability to generate conflict ideas or relationship arcs that align with popular tropes. For example, an AI prompt may suggest scenarios involving lovers with opposing goals or a misunderstanding that fuels romantic tension, providing the author with the building blocks for an emotionally engaging story.

Case Studies: Real-World Applications of AI Brainstorming Tools

Case Study 1: Building a Complex Mystery Plot

Mystery writer Emma Lawrence turned to AI brainstorming tools to craft a multifaceted murder mystery. Starting with a mind map, Lawrence identified each character's backstory, motives, and relationships with the victim, allowing her to visualize connections and potential conflicts. She then used an AI idea generator to develop red herrings and alibis, making each suspect's story plausible yet suspicious. This layering of clues and motives created a web of intrigue that kept readers guessing, and the AI's input enabled her to maintain a coherent, suspenseful structure throughout the narrative. By blending mind mapping and genre-specific prompts, Lawrence developed a mystery that was both complex and cohesive, providing an engaging experience for her readers.

Case Study 2: Exploring Multi-Dimensional Characters in Fantasy

Fantasy author Jon Palmer used AI brainstorming tools to explore his novel's intricate character dynamics. Palmer's story involved various factions with conflicting loyalties, and he wanted to ensure that each character's motives felt authentic. Using a mind map, he outlined each character's personal goals, alliances, and fears. Then, Palmer turned to an AI idea generator that suggested potential backstories and interpersonal conflicts based on keywords like "betrayal," "destiny," and "honor." One suggestion involved a character haunted by a past betrayal that influenced his alliance choices, adding complexity to Palmer's character arc. Through these tools, Palmer developed multi-dimensional characters whose decisions shaped the world-building and plot.

Case Study 3: Crafting Historical Accuracy in Historical Fiction

Historical fiction author Rachel Neumann, working on a novel set in Renaissance Italy, used genre-specific AI prompts to ensure historical accuracy. Neumann received prompts for period-appropriate settings, conflicts, and characters, including potential dialogue styles and mannerisms. When developing a character based on an artisan, for example, the AI suggested themes around guild politics and the influence of patronage on artistic expression. This prompt led Neumann to incorporate historical elements such as guild feuds and client-patron dynamics, adding a layer of authenticity to her story. By aligning her story with historical detail, she was able to create a vivid and engaging narrative that resonated with her readers.

Integrating AI Brainstorming Techniques into the Creative Process

By exploring these AI-powered brainstorming techniques, authors can navigate creative challenges with greater confidence and structure their stories more effectively. Mind mapping tools allow authors to visualize story elements and uncover relationships between characters, settings, and plotlines, while idea generators help authors expand initial ideas and create compelling story landscapes. Genre-specific prompts offer guidance on genre conventions, enhancing the realism and immersion that readers expect in specific genres.

These AI tools are particularly valuable in supporting authors at every stage of the creative process. By blending visual organization with dynamic prompts, authors can gain fresh insights, overcome creative blocks, and explore new angles on established story ideas. Ultimately, AI brainstorming tools don't just generate ideas; they facilitate a more fluid, imaginative creative process that allows authors to craft compelling, well-structured narratives that resonate with readers.

Case Studies of Successful AI-Assisted Idea Generation

Real-world case studies provide valuable insights into how authors use AI to enhance the creative process. By examining specific examples, authors can gain a deeper understanding of AI's practical benefits for overcoming blocks, refining ideas, and developing story elements.

Suspense Novelist Example: A suspense novelist, struggling with writer's block, used an AI tool to analyze popular crime novels. The AI tool identified common themes like psychological tension, unreliable narrators, and layered plot twists, guiding the author to incorporate similar elements. With these genre-specific insights, the author adapted foundational ideas to fit her unique voice, creating a suspenseful narrative that aligned with reader expectations. This AI support saved research time and offered tailored inspiration, making it easier to design a story that resonated with her audience.

Character Development Example: A fantasy author, finding it difficult to create multidimensional characters, used an AI-driven associative thinking tool to generate new traits and backstories. By inputting basic information, the tool suggested unique character arcs that included specific conflicts, backgrounds, and motivations. For instance, one character's narrative evolved to include a family feud shaping her worldview, which added depth and complexity. This AI-driven associative thinking approach enriched character interactions and enhanced the narrative, allowing the author to build a dynamic cast of characters that contributed to the story's thematic resonance.

Non-Fiction Topic Modeling Example: A non-fiction writer, working on a comprehensive guide to renewable energy, employed an AI topic modeling tool to organize her research. The AI analyzed vast data and presented cohesive clusters around themes like solar power, wind energy, and sustainable innovation. By highlighting connections between topics, the tool helped the author outline the book logically, ensuring clear progression and flow. This topic modeling tool not only clarified complex information but also saved the author significant time, resulting in a well-structured outline that streamlined the writing process.

These case studies illustrate AI's ability to support authors in crafting unique and successful projects by broadening perspectives and encouraging the exploration of new angles. Through practical examples, it's clear that AI-assisted idea generation can inspire innovative stories, strengthen narrative structure, and support character depth, helping authors confidently approach their creative work.

By embracing these AI-driven strategies, writers unlock new creative possibilities. This chapter explores the diverse ways AI can aid authors in finding inspiration, structuring ideas, and transforming abstract concepts into concrete story elements. Through AI's unique approach to idea generation, authors gain an invaluable tool for brainstorming, ensuring each project begins with a robust, imaginative foundation that resonates with readers.

Chapter 4: Research and Fact-Checking

In this chapter, we examine how AI can be an essential tool in the research and fact-checking stages of writing, providing authors with resources to gather, verify, and refine information efficiently. For authors working on non-fiction, research-intensive projects, or works that require factual accuracy, AI offers a valuable means to streamline information retrieval and ensure credibility. By exploring the range of AI tools available and understanding the nuances of their capabilities, authors can use these resources to enhance the depth and accuracy of their work.

AI Tools for Efficient Research

AI has transformed the research process for authors, equipping them with sophisticated tools that streamline information retrieval, data mining, and literature searches with unprecedented efficiency. For authors tackling complex topics, nonfiction subjects, or historically accurate fiction, these AI-powered tools provide crucial support by reducing time spent on manual searches and enabling quick access to credible, relevant information. By leveraging vast databases, scientific journals, historical archives, and other scholarly resources, AI allows authors to gather high-quality information and insights with ease, enhancing the depth, accuracy, and credibility of their work.

Efficient Information Retrieval

One of the primary advantages of AI in research is its ability to retrieve information rapidly and accurately. AI-driven research platforms can quickly scan multiple databases to locate specific data points, sources, and references based on keywords, phrases, dates, or events. This efficient retrieval saves authors from tedious manual searching and allows them to gather reliable information with minimal effort.

M.A.L.C.O.L.M.

Case Study: Historical Fiction Research

For authors writing historical fiction, the ability to pull up primary sources, articles, and visual resources from a specific time period is invaluable for creating an authentic narrative. Suppose an author is working on a novel set in 1920s New York. Using AI-powered research tools, they can:

Access news articles, personal diaries, and photographs from the 1920s, offering insights into language, social norms, and historical events of that period.

Locate primary source documents such as speeches, government records, and advertisements, providing accurate context for everyday life.

Integrate multimedia elements like photos and video clips to visualize and better understand the environment they're portraying.

Example: An author researching the cultural influence of jazz in Harlem during the 1920s can use AI to find newspaper articles on jazz clubs, biographies of famous musicians, and social commentaries from that time. This enables them to weave authentic details into the story, making the setting more vibrant and historically accurate.

Case Study: Scientific Research for Nonfiction

Nonfiction authors writing about scientific topics need access to the latest research findings to ensure their work is current and accurate. AI tools can pull data from specialized journals, databases, and scientific studies, enabling authors to integrate cutting-edge information.

Accessing Journals and Databases: An author writing on genetics can use AI tools to access recent studies on genomic research, CRISPR technology, or genetic counseling.

Keyword-Specific Results: By entering specific search terms like "gene therapy advancements 2023," the author can access focused, up-to-date information rather than sifting through unrelated data.

ARTIFICIAL INTELLIGENCE FOR AUTHORS

Citing Authoritative Sources: AI tools also provide proper citation formats and links to original studies, supporting the credibility of the author's work.

Example: A health writer using AI-driven research tools to explore the latest data on mental health treatments can access recent studies on therapies, medications, and innovative approaches. This allows them to produce a well-informed, authoritative piece that stands out in a rapidly evolving field.

Data Mining for Pattern Detection and Trend Analysis

AI tools equipped with data mining capabilities allow authors to detect patterns, correlations, and trends within large datasets. This feature is particularly valuable for authors working on data-driven topics like sociology, economics, and climate science, where analyzing statistical data and trends is essential for crafting compelling, evidence-based narratives.

Case Study: Data Analysis for Sociology

An author writing on urban development may want to explore how housing prices, population density, and infrastructure have evolved across various cities. With AI, they can:

Access datasets from multiple cities, covering housing prices, migration patterns, and income levels over time.

Analyze correlations between variables like income inequality and urban sprawl, helping to reveal how social and economic factors shape urban landscapes.

Identify trends over time and generate charts or visualizations that reinforce their arguments.

Example: A journalist using AI tools for data analysis might discover correlations between rising housing costs and reduced public transit access in certain metropolitan areas, offering a nuanced view of urban inequality.

Case Study: Environmental Data for Climate Science Writing

An author covering climate change can use AI to analyze environmental data such as temperature changes, carbon emissions, and deforestation rates across different regions and timeframes. This analysis helps the author to present a data-backed argument on climate trends.

Global Environmental Data: Access data on climate trends, CO_2 levels, and ocean temperatures across continents.

Visualize Trends: AI tools often include visualization options, helping authors create graphs and charts that highlight key findings.

Highlight Long-Term Impact: AI can analyze historical data to reveal long-term effects of climate policies on specific regions.

Example: A nonfiction author might use AI to compile a timeline of CO_2 emissions in the U.S. over the past 50 years, providing readers with a visual representation of the impact of policy changes on emissions.

AI-Powered Literature Search and Compilation

AI-driven literature search tools are revolutionizing the way authors locate academic articles, books, and studies. Instead of manually navigating through numerous databases or libraries, authors can use these tools to consolidate resources in one place, making it much easier to locate information on a specific topic.

Case Study: Psychology Research for Nonfiction

A nonfiction author writing about psychology may need to locate recent studies on cognitive behavior, neuroplasticity, or mental health trends. AI literature search tools help by:

Compiling recent studies on the chosen topic, consolidating results from multiple journals into a single list.

ARTIFICIAL INTELLIGENCE FOR AUTHORS

Categorizing findings by relevance, publication date, or source type, so authors can focus on the most pertinent research.

Providing citation support to ensure accurate sourcing and reduce the risk of plagiarism.

Example: A self-help author researching the effects of mindfulness on mental health can use AI to find recent articles, group them by type (e.g., meta-analyses, clinical trials), and create a reading list for deeper exploration.

Case Study: Historical Research for Fiction Writers

Historical fiction writers often need to verify cultural details, language use, fashion, or social customs from a specific period. Literature search tools streamline this process by offering centralized access to relevant resources.

Access Primary Source Materials: AI tools can help locate letters, diaries, or news articles from a specific historical era.

Cross-Reference Historical Facts: Literature search tools can link to historical archives and cultural studies, making it easier to verify dates, events, or social norms.

Easily Organized Findings: AI can organize search results by topic, event, or time period, creating a structured resource base for authors.

Example: A historical fiction writer working on a novel set in Victorian London can use AI to gather information on clothing styles, common slang, and popular literature of the time, bringing authenticity to their story.

Enhancing Credibility and Depth with AI Research Tools

AI research tools do more than just save time; they allow authors to deepen the accuracy, credibility, and richness of their work. By accessing specialized information, authors can provide evidence-based insights that resonate with readers. Whether authors are aiming to support arguments in nonfiction or enrich fictional worlds with realistic details, AI tools make this process far more manageable.

Case Study: Business Writing with Market Insights

A business writer developing a book on consumer behavior trends can leverage AI to access market reports, economic data, and industry whitepapers. This enables them to:

Identify consumer trends across demographics or regions, enhancing the accuracy of their insights.

Back claims with statistical evidence from reliable sources, reinforcing the credibility of their arguments.

Integrate recent findings on market shifts or emerging consumer habits, making the content timely and relevant.

Example: A business writer using AI research tools might access a report on e-commerce growth in the post-pandemic era, using the data to predict future trends in online retail for their readers..

Using AI to Verify Sources and Accuracy

Ensuring the credibility and accuracy of information is essential in both fiction and non-fiction writing. This verification process not only protects an author's reliability but also builds reader trust. With the proliferation of information available online, authors can sometimes find it challenging to determine which sources are credible and up-to-date. AI-powered tools offer sophisticated techniques to help authors verify sources, cross-reference data, and avoid misinformation, building a solid foundation for well-informed narratives and arguments. By using AI in the verification process, authors can improve the quality, integrity, and depth of their work.

Cross-Referencing Sources with AI

ARTIFICIAL INTELLIGENCE FOR AUTHORS

One of the primary benefits of AI in source verification is its ability to quickly cross-reference data across multiple databases and archives. This feature allows authors to identify discrepancies or inconsistencies in the information they're referencing, ensuring that each piece of data aligns with established facts or consensus. Cross-referencing tools can be particularly valuable for data-driven projects, where factual accuracy is paramount.

Case Study: Verifying Historical Facts for Fiction

Imagine an author writing a historical novel set during the American Civil War. They come across a fascinating anecdote about a real-life character who supposedly changed the course of a battle. Before including this detail, the author wants to verify its historical accuracy. AI tools can assist by:

Scanning multiple historical archives and military records to validate whether this character was indeed present at the battle in question.

Cross-referencing similar sources to check for consistency in dates, locations, and character involvement.

Flagging inconsistencies that might indicate the story is more folklore than fact.

Example: By using an AI-powered research tool, the author discovers that although the character did participate in the battle, the anecdote's details are exaggerated in certain sources. This allows the author to portray the character more accurately, creating a more authentic narrative.

Case Study: Data Validation for Non-Fiction

For non-fiction authors, accuracy is critical, especially when dealing with scientific or statistical data. Suppose an author writing a book on renewable energy wants to reference data on solar panel efficiency trends. AI can assist by:

Cross-checking data across scientific journals and industry reports to ensure the statistics are up-to-date and widely accepted.

Highlighting potential discrepancies between sources, which may signal that some sources use outdated or context-specific data.

Providing additional sources that reinforce or dispute the findings, helping the author build a balanced view.

Example: An author working on renewable energy trends finds conflicting data on solar efficiency improvements. AI tools help by cross-referencing more recent studies, ensuring the author presents the most accurate information to their readers.

Evaluating Source Credibility with AI

Advanced AI tools can assess a source's credibility by analyzing factors like publication date, author credentials, and peer reviews. This feature is especially beneficial for authors covering scientific, academic, or policy-focused topics, where referencing credible sources is crucial. AI can help distinguish between high-quality sources and those that may lack authority or present biased perspectives.

Case Study: Assessing Source Quality for a Scientific Book

An author writing a book on neuroscience needs to ensure their sources are credible, as they're discussing complex concepts that require accurate, peer-reviewed information. By using an AI credibility-checking tool, they can:

Identify the author's credentials for each source, determining if the writer is an expert in neuroscience or a related field.

Check if the study has been peer-reviewed, indicating that it has undergone scrutiny by other experts.

Evaluate the publication's reputation, helping the author avoid sources from journals with weak standards or controversial affiliations.

Example: The AI tool flags a study on brain plasticity that lacks peer review and was published by an unfamiliar journal. The author decides to rely on other, more credible sources, ensuring their work maintains a high standard of scientific rigor.

Example: Filtering Credible News for a Current Events Book

An author writing about climate change policy wants to incorporate recent government and industry news but needs to ensure their sources are reliable. AI tools can evaluate the credibility of news sources by analyzing:

Publication reputation and historical accuracy in covering scientific news.

Author credentials to confirm the writer's expertise in climate science or policy.

Bias detection to identify any sources that may present skewed viewpoints.

Example: AI identifies that an article from a lesser-known outlet shows clear bias, allowing the author to choose an alternative, credible source, thereby strengthening their argument's neutrality.

Detecting Misinformation with AI

In an era of widespread misinformation, it's essential for authors to verify controversial or widely debated information. AI tools that detect misinformation can compare statements against verified sources and flag content that deviates from established facts. This is especially useful for authors tackling sensitive topics such as politics, public health, and environmental issues.

Case Study: Avoiding Misinformation in a Health Book

Suppose an author is writing a book on nutrition and wellness and encounters a statistic that contradicts current scientific consensus. By using AI's misinformation detection feature, the author can:

Compare the statistic with reliable sources such as peer-reviewed journals and government health databases.

Receive warnings if the information is flagged as misleading or based on outdated research.

Access more reliable data from verified sources to replace the potentially misleading statistic.

Example: The AI tool flags a statistic on dietary supplements, pointing out that recent studies dispute its validity. The author revises the section, using the latest research to ensure accuracy.

Example: Verifying Controversial Claims for a Political Book

An author writing a book on global politics wants to cite data on government surveillance programs. Given the controversial nature of the topic, they use an AI tool to cross-reference claims with government reports and investigative journalism.

Identify reliable sources like verified reports from international agencies or reputable investigative outlets.

Flag inconsistencies where certain claims do not align with available evidence.

Suggest alternative, well-documented data to maintain the credibility of the author's work.

Example: The AI tool highlights that certain information on surveillance is largely speculative. The author opts to rely on reports from reputable agencies, ensuring their book presents well-supported arguments.

Filtering Sources for Relevance with AI

ARTIFICIAL INTELLIGENCE FOR AUTHORS

In addition to verifying accuracy, AI tools can also evaluate source relevance by determining how closely a source aligns with an author's topic. This filtering capability saves time by allowing authors to focus on the most relevant sources that contribute meaningfully to their narrative or argument.

Case Study: Refining Sources for an Economics Book

An author writing about income inequality encounters numerous studies, some of which are tangentially related to their topic but lack the specificity needed for direct support. AI tools can help by:

Filtering out less relevant studies, such as those focusing on other aspects of economics that don't directly contribute to the topic of inequality.

Prioritizing sources that specifically address income distribution, taxation, or economic mobility.

Highlighting recent studies to ensure the author's work is informed by current research.

Example: The AI tool filters the research list, providing the author with studies directly focused on income inequality trends. This focus improves the book's depth and accuracy without wasting time on loosely related material.

Example: Curating Sources for a Cultural History Book

An author writing about 20th-century art movements needs references that are both historically accurate and relevant to specific art forms. AI can assist by:

Filtering out sources that don't pertain to the art movements in question, such as unrelated cultural studies.

Sorting sources by date, allowing the author to access materials specific to the time period.

Highlighting influential publications, ensuring the author references the most significant works.

Example: The AI tool curates a list of resources focused on influential art movements, helping the author create a more informed and cohesive narrative without excessive searching.

Enhancing Credibility and Depth with AI Verification Tools

By employing AI-powered source verification techniques, authors gain confidence in the credibility and accuracy of their research. This assurance enables them to create well-supported arguments and in-depth narratives that resonate with readers. Additionally, AI tools can strengthen the research process by:

Filtering unreliable sources, allowing authors to focus on high-quality information.

Providing real-time alerts for misinformation or outdated data, ensuring their work is timely and relevant.

Organizing relevant sources based on relevance and specificity, saving time and improving content quality.

Example: Building a Balanced Argument in a Nonfiction Book on Renewable Energy

An author writing on renewable energy sources wants to include a balanced view of the advantages and limitations of solar power. With AI tools, they can:

Identify reputable sources that provide both positive and critical perspectives, ensuring a balanced presentation.

Flag biased or unverified sources, allowing the author to avoid controversial claims without evidence.

Filter research by recent advancements, helping the author stay current with emerging technology.

Avoiding Pitfalls of AI-Generated Information

While AI is a powerful tool for research, data analysis, and idea generation, it is essential for authors to be aware of its limitations to avoid potential pitfalls. As advanced as AI models are, they still rely on pre-existing datasets for training, which can lead to inherent biases, outdated information, and oversimplification in the suggestions, summaries, or interpretations they provide. By understanding these limitations, authors can ensure they use AI responsibly and effectively, ultimately producing work that is factually accurate, balanced, and nuanced.

1. Recognizing and Mitigating Bias in AI-Generated Information

AI models are trained on vast datasets, often collected from sources across the internet and publications. However, these datasets frequently reflect dominant cultural and societal biases, especially when they come predominantly from Western or English-language sources. This can lead to unintentional skewed perspectives in the information AI provides, which can impact an author's work.

Case Study: Cultural Bias in Historical Research

Imagine an author writing a historical novel set in colonial India, aiming to depict a balanced perspective on the colonial impact on Indian society. An AI tool trained on Western sources may:

Overemphasize colonial viewpoints, downplaying the local Indian perspectives or cultural nuances.

Highlight British narratives and policies without providing insights into local resistance movements or the effects on indigenous communities.

Example: By relying solely on AI-generated summaries, the author may inadvertently portray a colonial perspective as the primary lens, losing the cultural richness of Indian society. To mitigate this, the author could supplement AI-generated information with primary sources from Indian authors and local archives to ensure a balanced representation.

Case Study: Gender Bias in Scientific Writing

Suppose an author is writing a non-fiction book on technology trends and relies on AI tools to gather information about leading figures and groundbreaking studies. Due to historical gender biases in tech, AI might:

Predominantly showcase male inventors, developers, or CEOs, neglecting the contributions of women and underrepresented groups in the field.

Reflect biases in source material that can result in an incomplete portrayal of the tech industry's diversity.

Example: If the AI-generated information lacks diversity in representation, the author could proactively seek additional sources that highlight contributions from a wider range of voices. This approach ensures that their work celebrates diverse perspectives and acknowledges historically overlooked contributors.

2. Limitations in Accessing Up-to-Date Information

AI models trained on static datasets may lack the most recent information, especially for fields like science, technology, current events, or public policy that evolve rapidly. Authors relying solely on AI-generated insights may risk incorporating outdated information, which can impact the accuracy of their work.

Case Study: Outdated Data in Scientific Writing

An author writing about gene-editing advancements may encounter limitations with AI-generated information, as these technologies evolve quickly and require the latest research to remain accurate. Using outdated data could:

Misrepresent the current state of gene-editing technology, leaving out critical breakthroughs or regulatory changes.

Impact credibility if readers identify newer information that contradicts the author's claims.

Example: The author supplements AI research with recent scientific journals, databases like PubMed, and direct access to peer-reviewed articles to confirm that their information aligns with the latest findings, ensuring credibility.

Case Study: Political Analysis and Current Events

A journalist or author analyzing political trends might use AI to gather background information, but if the AI is trained on older data, it may:

Miss recent legislative changes, elections, or shifts in public opinion, impacting the relevance and accuracy of the analysis.

Present an outdated picture that does not account for recent developments in geopolitics or public sentiment.

Example: By cross-referencing AI-generated information with reputable news sources, such as Reuters, BBC, or AP News, the author can verify that their political analysis remains current and relevant.

Oversimplification and Loss of Nuance

AI-generated summaries, while efficient, often lack the depth and complexity that human researchers can provide. This is especially problematic in areas requiring a deep understanding of context, cultural nuances, or specialized knowledge. An AI-generated summary may overlook subtle conditions, qualifications, or limitations of certain studies or historical facts, which could lead to a misrepresentation of information.

Case Study: Simplified Psychological Study Summaries

Consider an author writing about mental health who uses AI tools to summarize psychological studies. AI might generate summaries that:

Omit the specific conditions under which the study's results were achieved, such as sample size, participant demographics, or limitations acknowledged by the researchers.

Neglect contextual factors that impact the study's findings, potentially leading to overgeneralizations.

Example: The AI summary of a study on cognitive behavior therapy (CBT) might omit that the study was conducted on a specific age group or in a clinical setting, which limits the general applicability of the findings. The author would benefit from consulting the full study to ensure their work accurately represents the research.

Case Study: Historical Nuance in Cultural Studies

For a historical fiction writer, AI-generated summaries of historical events might overlook important cultural contexts or societal norms that shaped those events. This can lead to an oversimplified portrayal of complex historical moments.

Contextual details such as economic conditions, regional dialects, or social customs may be excluded in favor of general summaries.

Missed nuances in social hierarchies or cultural dynamics might result in an inaccurate or stereotypical depiction.

Example: An author writing about life in 19th-century China might find AI summaries too broad, omitting key aspects of class structures or Confucian values that shaped social interactions. To capture these nuances, the author could consult primary historical records, memoirs, or specialized academic studies.

Best Practices for Using AI While Avoiding Pitfalls

To mitigate these limitations, authors should treat AI as a supplement to traditional research methods rather than a replacement. This approach allows them to harness AI's efficiency while cross-referencing, verifying, and contextualizing the information it provides.

1. Cross-Referencing AI-Generated Insights with Reputable Primary Sources

Authors should validate AI-generated information by comparing it with reputable primary sources, such as academic databases, established journals, and verified archival materials. This cross-referencing can help identify discrepancies, ensuring that AI-generated insights are reliable.

Example: If an AI suggests a historical detail, the author could verify it using primary sources like government records, archived newspapers, or expert-authored histories to confirm accuracy.

2. Consulting Multiple AI Tools and Traditional Databases

Using multiple AI tools or combining AI with traditional research resources can broaden an author's perspective. Each AI tool might be trained on different datasets, providing varied angles on the same topic, which can reduce the likelihood of bias or gaps in information.

Example: An author researching global economic trends could use one AI tool for general information, another for industry-specific insights, and complement these findings with data from traditional databases like World Bank, OECD, or IMF.

3. Critically Assessing the Accuracy and Relevance of AI's Output

Authors should apply a critical lens to AI-generated content, evaluating it for potential oversimplifications, outdated details, or contextual gaps. Reviewing the AI's output in light of the topic's complexity can help ensure that the final product is both nuanced and accurate.

Example: When AI provides a summary of a scientific study, the author can critically assess whether the summary includes study limitations, sample demographics, and methodological nuances that impact the findings.

4. Supplementing AI Insights with Expert Perspectives

For complex topics or specialized fields, authors can supplement AI insights with direct input from experts or by consulting recent peer-reviewed studies. This approach allows authors to enrich their work with expert commentary and ensures that nuanced perspectives are not lost.

Example: An author writing about cybersecurity could enhance AI-generated information by interviewing cybersecurity professionals or reviewing reports from trusted organizations like MITRE or the Cybersecurity and Infrastructure Security Agency (CISA).

Chapter 5: Character Development and World-Building

In this chapter, we explore how AI can be a powerful tool for authors in the crucial stages of character development and world-building. By using AI to generate unique characters, build immersive settings, and delve into character motivations and relationships, writers can add depth and complexity to their stories, creating memorable narratives that resonate with readers. With AI's ability to generate details and simulate scenarios, authors gain a valuable resource that helps them flesh out their characters and the worlds they inhabit in new and innovative ways.

AI-Assisted Character Creation

Developing unique, memorable characters is fundamental to storytelling, as well-drawn characters drive emotional engagement and bring the narrative to life. AI-powered tools offer authors innovative methods to generate, shape, and deepen their characters through various features that suggest personality traits, backstories, motivations, and even complex relationship dynamics. By assisting in character creation, AI enables authors to efficiently explore and build layered personalities that captivate readers and drive the story forward.

1. Generating Detailed Character Profiles

One of the most powerful ways AI supports authors is by creating comprehensive character profiles that serve as foundational sketches for authors to build upon. These profiles often include core elements such as background, motivations, and psychological traits that help an author understand how a character might act and evolve throughout the story.

Case Study: Using AI to Develop a Protagonist's Backstory

Consider an author writing a fantasy novel with a protagonist who grew up in a secluded, mystical forest. The AI tool could generate a profile that includes the character's childhood experiences, education, and family dynamics, providing the foundation for their worldview and emotional drivers. The profile might include:

Childhood Experiences: The protagonist, who was raised by an eccentric hermit, learned self-reliance from an early age.

Family Dynamics: They have a complex relationship with their only family member, a reclusive parent figure who instilled in them both wisdom and fear of the outside world.

Ambitions and Fears: Despite their sheltered life, they long for adventure but are haunted by a fear of rejection and failure.

Example: By providing this level of detail, the AI allows the author to build a character who feels real and grounded. The protagonist's background informs their hesitations, relationships, and responses to challenges, allowing the story's progression to feel authentic and emotionally resonant.

2. Trait and Archetype Suggestions for Dynamic Characters

Many AI tools offer trait and archetype suggestions to help authors create characters with distinctive attributes, strengths, and flaws. These tools can recommend traits that fit well-known archetypes—like the reluctant hero, the wise mentor, or the anti-hero—and also suggest ways to expand, combine, or subvert these archetypes for originality.

Case Study: Creating a Complex Anti-Hero

An author working on a thriller decides to write an anti-hero protagonist. The AI suggests blending charming but morally gray traits such as resourcefulness mixed with a lack of empathy, creating a character who is both compelling and flawed.

Positive Traits: The protagonist is charismatic, brave, and clever.

Challenges: They struggle with a lack of empathy and are driven by self-interest, which leads them into morally ambiguous situations.

Internal Conflict: The AI suggests that while the character is skilled at manipulation, they harbor an unspoken desire for genuine connection.

Example: This nuanced profile allows the author to explore the protagonist's journey of transformation. As the story progresses, the character's charm draws readers in, but their questionable morals keep them on edge, adding complexity to the plot.

Example: Subverting Archetypes in a Romance Novel

An author writing a romance novel can use AI to play with traditional character archetypes, such as the "stoic love interest." Instead of a cold exterior, the AI suggests the character's distance comes from a fear of vulnerability rooted in past heartbreak. This subversion offers depth and an opportunity for the character's arc to evolve naturally, creating a more compelling, layered personality.

3. Psychological Profiling for Realistic Behavior and Reactions

AI tools often incorporate psychological profiling that helps authors understand how characters might respond to specific situations or interact with others. This feature can generate personality-driven prompts that allow authors to portray characters in ways that feel psychologically consistent and true to life.

Case Study: Navigating Insecurity and Ambition in a Young Leader

Imagine an author writing a science fiction novel where the main character is a young, ambitious leader struggling with insecurity. The AI can generate prompts and scenarios that explore how these traits interact, such as:

Suggested Scenarios: The character's drive for success leads them to make a risky decision that strains relationships with their team.

Behavioral Prompts: When faced with doubt from others, the AI suggests that the character might respond defensively, masking their insecurity with arrogance.

Long-Term Growth: The AI recommends a journey where the character learns to balance confidence with humility, evolving from a defensive leader to a respected one.

Example: This insight into the character's psychology allows the author to portray a rich internal struggle, enhancing the character's relatability and making their journey feel earned.

Example: Leveraging Personality Types in a Mystery Novel

An author working on a mystery novel could use AI to assign specific personality traits based on Myers-Briggs or Enneagram types, enhancing their understanding of each character's motivations and blind spots. For a character who is introverted and detail-oriented, the AI might suggest scenarios where their attentiveness helps solve clues, but their hesitation to engage with others slows the investigation, adding realism to their role.

4. Adding Quirks and Unique Traits for Memorable Characters

AI tools can generate quirks and distinctive traits that bring characters to life and make them feel relatable. These small, seemingly inconsequential details can add layers to a character's personality and serve as symbols, plot devices, or character-revealing moments.

Case Study: Using AI to Add Relatable Quirks

An author writing a young adult novel might want to add relatable quirks to their characters. The AI could suggest details like:

Hobbies or Collections: A character who collects old postcards from around the world, hinting at a desire for adventure.

Unique Behaviors: A protagonist who sings quietly when nervous, adding charm to their interactions.

Subtle Phobias: A character who feels uneasy on sunny days due to a childhood trauma, subtly influencing their mood.

Example: These quirks not only make the characters more interesting but also create connections with readers who recognize their own idiosyncrasies in the characters.

Example: Using Quirks as Plot Devices in Fantasy

In a fantasy setting, AI might suggest that a character keeps a hidden journal of ancient spells. This quirk not only makes them more memorable but can serve as a plot device, unlocking key information at a critical moment in the story.

5. Building Character Dynamics and Relationship Conflicts

For ensemble casts, AI can help authors envision character dynamics and potential conflicts that arise from personality clashes, shared goals, or contrasting backgrounds. These dynamics enrich the story by adding interpersonal tension and complexity to the relationships.

Case Study: Creating a Tense Mentor-Student Dynamic

An author writing an adventure novel with a mentor-student relationship might use AI to explore potential conflicts, such as:

Conflicting Worldviews: The AI suggests that the mentor values tradition, while the student embraces innovation, leading to tension.

Emotional Blockages: The student's rebellious streak and impatience frustrate the mentor's disciplined approach.

Resolution: Over time, they learn to value each other's perspectives, with the student bringing new ideas and the mentor offering wisdom.

Example: This dynamic adds depth to the story, giving readers a satisfying arc of conflict, growth, and resolution in the relationship.

Example: Generating Romantic Tension in a Drama

An author working on a drama may want to create a romantic relationship fraught with tension. AI can suggest that one character's fear of vulnerability clashes with the other's need for openness. This conflict adds stakes to the relationship and allows for a realistic exploration of personal growth and compromise.

6. Crafting Authentic Dialogue Through AI Prompts

AI tools can assist authors in crafting authentic dialogue that reflects each character's unique voice and personality, ensuring conversations feel natural and true to character. Dialogue prompts can incorporate specific traits, emotional cues, and conversational styles based on a character's personality.

Case Study: Dialogue for a Shy, Intelligent Character in a Thriller

If an author has developed a character who is shy but highly observant, AI might suggest dialogue prompts that:

Use minimal, precise language that hints at intelligence while avoiding emotional vulnerability.

Display nervous habits in their speech patterns, such as trailing off or second-guessing statements.

Avoid direct confrontation in favor of indirect suggestions, reflecting their aversion to conflict.

Example: This level of character-driven dialogue creates a realistic portrayal, making conversations feel more immersive and engaging for readers.

Example: Sarcastic Banter in a Romantic Comedy

For a romantic comedy, the AI might suggest that a character frequently uses sarcasm as a defense mechanism. This gives the author a framework to write witty banter and playful insults that add humor and reveal layers of personality, establishing a unique relationship dynamic.

Generating Unique Worlds and Settings

World-Building is an essential part of storytelling, especially in genres like fantasy, science fiction, and historical fiction where the setting often plays a central role. A richly developed world not only provides a backdrop but also influences plot dynamics, character motivations, and thematic depth, functioning almost as a character in itself. AI-powered tools have emerged as invaluable resources for authors, offering powerful assistance in the complex task of world-building by generating geographical layouts, cultural elements, historical contexts, and intricate details that make fictional worlds feel as real and immersive as our own.

1. Building Geographical Foundations with AI

Geography serves as the physical foundation of any fictional world. AI tools can assist authors in creating diverse landscapes that shape the characters' lives, influence travel and trade, and contribute to cultural distinctions within the story. With AI, authors can map out terrains like mountains, rivers, forests, and cities, visualizing the spatial relationships between different areas.

Case Study: Mapping a Fantasy Continent for Epic Adventures

Consider an author working on an epic fantasy novel set in a vast, unexplored continent. Using AI tools, they can generate a map that includes a variety of ecosystems and climatic regions:

Lush Jungles and Arid Deserts: Each with distinct flora and fauna, offering unique resources, challenges, and environments for characters to explore.

Snow-Covered Peaks and Fertile Valleys: Creating natural boundaries between regions, fostering different ways of life and influencing cultural development.

Urban Landscapes and Small Villages: AI can suggest city layouts that emphasize trade or defense, while villages may focus on agriculture or resource gathering.

Example: The AI might suggest a trade route passing through perilous mountains and dense forests, which could become a key setting for encounters with bandits, creating natural obstacles for the protagonist. These geographical elements provide opportunities for plot development and enrich the story by adding environmental challenges and cultural diversity across the regions.

Example: Visualizing the World for a Dystopian Future

For a science fiction novel set in a post-apocalyptic Earth, an AI could help create a landscape transformed by climate change, with abandoned cities, encroaching deserts, and isolated safe zones. This bleak geography would set the tone, showing readers the devastating effects of a failed society and influencing the characters' daily struggles for survival.

2. Designing Cultural and Societal Structures with AI

Beyond physical landscapes, cultures and societies make fictional worlds feel lived-in. AI tools can help authors craft unique customs, traditions, belief systems, and societal norms that define the people inhabiting the world. By suggesting elements like festivals, attire, social roles, and etiquette, AI assists in creating cultures that feel both authentic and immersive.

Case Study: Creating a Complex Society with Diverse Traditions

An author writing about a multi-ethnic empire in a fantasy setting may use AI to develop cultural practices and social dynamics unique to each group within the empire. For example:

Distinct Festivals: Each culture might have its own seasonal festivals celebrating harvests, historical victories, or religious holidays, adding depth to the world and creating natural plot points for characters from different backgrounds to interact.

Food and Attire: The AI could suggest traditional dishes and clothing styles that reflect each culture's environment, resources, and values, making the world feel cohesive and well-rounded.

Family Structures and Social Roles: AI tools might generate ideas for matriarchal clans in one region and a guild-based society in another, allowing for diverse social structures that can create interesting social dynamics and conflicts.

Example: The author could use these cultural elements to fuel inter-group conflicts, misunderstandings, or alliances, which add tension and complexity to the plot. For instance, a character from a nomadic tribe might struggle to adapt to the rigid hierarchy of the empire's capital, providing a subplot about cultural identity and adaptation.

3. Developing Historical Contexts and Timelines

AI tools can assist authors in creating historical backgrounds and timelines that give a fictional world depth and continuity. A strong historical context can include pivotal events like wars, revolutions, alliances, and discoveries that shape the world's present-day politics, social norms, and technological advancements.

Case Study: Building a Timeline of Technological Evolution in Science Fiction

A science fiction author writing about a future society on a distant planet might use AI to develop a timeline of key technological advancements and political shifts that explain how humanity reached this point:

Milestones in Space Travel and Terraforming: AI could suggest breakthroughs that allowed humans to colonize other planets, including key figures and inventions that catalyzed these changes.

Historical Conflicts and Alliances: A timeline of conflicts with alien civilizations or rival human colonies could explain existing power dynamics and cultural mistrust.

Shifts in Social Structure: AI might propose events like revolutions or migrations that led to the formation of distinct communities with unique languages, religions, and customs.

Example: The author uses this timeline to create a rich backstory for the colony, including legends of the first settlers and cultural myths that influence characters' beliefs and actions. This historical depth enhances the narrative by giving characters a legacy and a set of traditions that feel natural and authentic.

Example: Legendary Conflicts in a Fantasy World

For a fantasy author, AI can help create a mythical past filled with legendary battles, alliances, and betrayals that influence current events. For instance:

Ancient Kingdoms and Rivalries: AI might suggest long-forgotten kingdoms and rivalries that influence the current rulers' decisions.

Relics and Artifacts: Ancient objects, spells, or prophecies could serve as plot devices, influencing the protagonist's quest or creating conflict among factions seeking the same relic.

Example: The author can use these historical elements to create a sense of destiny or fate for the protagonist, as they navigate a world still shaped by the actions of ancient heroes and villains.

4. Crafting Political Structures and Power Dynamics

Political structures and social hierarchies add layers of tension and complexity to a fictional world. AI can help authors design governments, legal systems, and social classes that create the conditions for conflict, alliances, and character motivations.

Case Study: Designing a World with Interconnected Factions

ARTIFICIAL INTELLIGENCE FOR AUTHORS

An author writing a dystopian novel might use AI to create a setting where various factions, such as a military junta, a coalition of rogue scientists, and a powerful tech corporation, compete for control:

Military Rule: The AI could suggest laws that prioritize order and obedience, creating conflicts with other factions who oppose these strictures.

Corporate Influence: The tech corporation's power allows them to control essential resources, giving them leverage over citizens and other factions.

Rebel Scientists: Scientists working to restore ecological balance are labeled as threats, creating an underground resistance.

Example: The author can use these power dynamics to fuel the plot, with characters caught in the crossfire of these powerful groups, each representing different ideologies about how society should be run.

Example: Constructing a Feudal Society in a Fantasy Setting

In a fantasy world, AI could help an author design a feudal kingdom with a strict class hierarchy, including:

Nobles, Merchants, and Serfs: Each class with distinct roles and privileges, leading to tensions over wealth, land ownership, and influence.

Religious and Political Conflicts: A powerful religious order might compete with the monarchy, creating conflict and alliances among nobles loyal to different factions.

Example: The author could create character arcs around social mobility, as characters try to escape their caste, climb the social ladder, or challenge the existing hierarchy.

5. Exploring Alternate Histories and Futuristic Scenarios

AI tools can help authors create alternate histories or futuristic worlds by simulating how certain historical events or technological advancements might have changed society.

Case Study: Speculative World-Building in a "What-If" Scenario

For an author writing speculative fiction about a world where steam technology became dominant, AI can help create a realistic progression of events that shape this alternate timeline:

Advanced Steam Machines: AI suggests inventions that improve industry and transportation, creating an industrialized society with steam-powered vehicles and factories.

Social and Environmental Effects: AI might propose how this technology impacted the environment, class structures, and even art forms, reflecting the values of a steam-centric society.

Example: The author's world feels consistent and believable because the AI provides logical progressions and implications of this technological choice, adding realism to the "what-if" scenario.

6. Adding Unique Details: Languages, Architecture, and Beliefs

To fully immerse readers, AI tools can assist with the smaller details that make a world come alive, including languages, religious beliefs, architecture, and everyday customs.

Case Study: Developing Regional Dialects and Languages

An author writing a high fantasy novel with multiple regions might use AI to suggest linguistic traits unique to each area:

Dialectical Variations: Characters from different regions might use distinct phrases or slang, adding realism to dialogues.

Conlang (Constructed Language): For advanced world-building, AI might assist in creating basic grammar and vocabulary for an entirely new language.

Example: A character's way of speaking could reveal their origin or social status, enriching the dialogue and adding authenticity to character interactions.

Example: Creating Culturally Reflective Architecture

AI could suggest architectural styles that align with a society's values, such as ornate temples in a religious society or towering skyscrapers for an economic powerhouse. This detail adds thematic depth by visually representing the society's priorities.

Example: In a dystopian setting, a city's architecture might feature defensive walls, guard towers, and militarized zones, reflecting a society obsessed with security and control.

Using AI to Explore Character Motivations and Relationships

In storytelling, character motivations, psychology, and relationship dynamics are essential for creating narratives that feel emotionally authentic and resonate deeply with readers. Characters who possess clear, consistent motivations and have complex, believable interactions add depth to a story, transforming it into a compelling exploration of human behavior. AI tools offer valuable support to authors by helping them delve deeper into character motivations and relationships, leading to richer, more authentic character arcs and multi-dimensional connections between characters.

1. Analyzing and Developing Character Motivations

A character's motivations drive their actions, shape their decisions, and influence how they interact with others. AI tools can help authors explore the psychological foundations of these motivations by analyzing backgrounds, personality traits, and life experiences to suggest underlying desires, fears, and ambitions.

Case Study: Exploring a Protagonist's Need for Validation

Imagine an author creating a protagonist who is a highly ambitious lawyer. With input about the character's background (e.g., they grew up in a family that prioritized academic achievement), an AI tool could:

Suggest underlying motives, such as a need for validation and fear of failure due to high parental expectations.

Explore the impact of past experiences, like a traumatic early loss in a case, which might drive them to win at any cost to prove their competence.

Highlight vulnerabilities related to self-worth, such as a tendency to overwork or a reluctance to accept help.

Example: With these insights, the author can depict the character's ambition as a double-edged sword, fueling both their success and their insecurities. This understanding allows the author to portray the protagonist's relentless drive in a way that feels realistic and adds psychological depth to their journey.

Example: Creating a Character with Trust Issues

An author writing a romance novel could use AI to develop a character with a strong fear of intimacy and commitment due to past heartbreak. By inputting details about the character's past relationships, the AI might suggest:

Subtle behavioral patterns, such as withdrawing when conversations become too personal or sabotaging relationships when they get too close.

Conflicting desires, as the character yearns for connection but is held back by the fear of being hurt again.

Opportunities for growth, where the character might slowly open up as they learn to trust a new romantic partner.

Example: This exploration of trust issues gives the author a roadmap for creating realistic emotional hurdles and breakthroughs, making the romance feel genuine and earned.

2. Simulating Character Growth and Transformation

Character growth is often a central theme in storytelling, as readers enjoy watching characters evolve in response to their experiences. AI tools can suggest psychologically plausible paths for character development, helping authors map out how a character might grow, change, or resist transformation over time.

Case Study: A Timid Character's Journey to Assertiveness

Suppose an author's protagonist starts the story as a timid, conflict-averse individual. The AI could suggest a series of events that gradually build their confidence:

Early challenges that push the character slightly out of their comfort zone, helping them practice assertiveness in small ways.

Catalyst events, such as standing up to an antagonist, which become turning points for developing bravery.

Subtle, ongoing struggles with doubt and fear that keep the growth process realistic and engaging for readers.

Example: The AI might propose that the character's assertiveness grows as they gain allies who believe in them, adding complexity to their journey. This transformation feels authentic because it is grounded in both internal growth and external support, creating a character arc that resonates with readers.

Example: Maintaining Flaws in an Anti-Hero's Arc

An author working on a psychological thriller may want an anti-hero who grows in some respects but remains flawed. The AI could suggest that the character becomes more skilled in dealing with conflicts and manipulative situations, yet retains selfish tendencies and an inability to empathize fully. This nuanced growth allows the character to change without losing their essential anti-hero qualities, making the arc feel both realistic and suspenseful.

3. Exploring Complex Character Dynamics and Interpersonal Relationships

Relationships add richness to a story, as they allow readers to see different aspects of characters through their interactions. AI tools can help authors create character dynamics and potential conflicts or alliances by analyzing personalities, values, and backgrounds to suggest how characters complement or clash with one another.

Case Study: Building a Rivals-to-Allies Relationship in a Fantasy Story

Consider an author creating a fantasy adventure with two characters who start as rivals. AI tools can help shape this dynamic by suggesting points of friction and potential alliance:

Differing goals: The AI might note that one character seeks personal glory, while the other is focused on protecting their community, leading to philosophical clashes.

Shared experiences: As the characters face a mutual threat, the AI might suggest specific events where they rely on each other, fostering mutual respect and shifting their relationship.

Gradual resolution of differences: The AI could propose how their competitive tension gradually transforms into camaraderie and mutual loyalty.

Example: These suggestions allow the author to develop a relationship arc that evolves naturally from rivalry to teamwork, enhancing the emotional stakes of the story.

Example: Friendships with Clashing Personality Types

An author writing a contemporary drama might explore a friendship between a pragmatic, analytical character and an idealistic, emotionally driven one. The AI could suggest:

Areas of friction, such as disagreements over problem-solving approaches, with one character preferring logical solutions while the other values empathy.

Moments of support, as each character brings a needed perspective that balances the other, leading to growth in their relationship.

Breakdowns and reconciliations, where intense disagreements test the friendship, only to ultimately strengthen it.

Example: By exploring these dynamics, the author can create a friendship that feels authentic and enduring, with moments of conflict and reconciliation that add depth to the story.

4. Generating Conflicts and Alliances Based on Individual Traits

AI can suggest character conflicts and alliances by analyzing personality traits, values, and past experiences. These suggestions can help authors create relationships that feel inevitable yet complex, with interactions that drive the story forward.

Case Study: Tension Between Two Strong-Willed Characters

For an action-adventure novel, an author might create two characters who are both ambitious and headstrong. The AI could suggest that their similar traits lead to conflicts over leadership and decision-making, but they eventually realize their shared goals create a powerful alliance:

Initial conflicts: Clashes over who should lead their team, with neither willing to compromise.

Shared challenges: As they encounter difficult situations, they recognize each other's strengths, gradually developing mutual respect.

Final alliance: An AI-generated suggestion might be that a common enemy forces them to cooperate, creating a bond based on their shared strengths and ideals.

Example: The author uses this framework to show that while the characters may clash due to similar traits, they ultimately create a formidable team, adding layers of tension and resolution to the narrative.

Example: Complicated Romantic Tension with Opposing Goals

In a romantic subplot, an AI might suggest two characters who share undeniable chemistry but have conflicting goals—such as one seeking a stable life and the other desiring adventure. These differences could lead to:

Conflicting values: The characters' divergent life paths create an obstacle to their relationship, adding tension and emotional stakes.

Moments of vulnerability: The AI could propose moments where each character briefly considers the other's viewpoint, creating a sense of mutual respect despite their differences.

A bittersweet ending: The AI might suggest a resolution where the characters part ways to pursue their individual goals, creating a powerful, emotionally resonant ending.

Example: This relationship arc provides both romantic tension and a realistic portrayal of incompatible values, making the story more complex and poignant.

5. Understanding Character Influence and Emotional Interconnection

Characters don't exist in isolation; their growth, setbacks, and decisions impact the people around them. AI tools can help authors explore the psychological effects of one character's actions on others, fostering a story where relationships feel interconnected and dynamic.

Case Study: Impact of a Character's Transformation on Others

Suppose a central character in a crime drama undergoes a major transformation, from a morally gray figure to a more ethical, responsible person. AI could suggest:

Jealousy from allies: Former partners in crime may feel resentment as the protagonist changes, creating tension and testing loyalties.

Admiration and support: Close friends or a love interest might encourage this change, bringing emotional support and helping the protagonist stay on their new path.

Reluctant acceptance: The AI might suggest a rival who is initially skeptical but gradually respects the protagonist's transformation, leading to an unexpected alliance.

Example: These dynamics allow the author to show the ripple effect of the protagonist's growth, where others respond in ways that add complexity to the relationships and deepen the story's emotional impact.

Example: How a Character's Downfall Affects Their Family

In a family drama, AI can help explore how one character's destructive behavior impacts their relatives. The AI might suggest:

Feelings of betrayal: Siblings or parents may feel hurt or betrayed, leading to strained family ties and moments of confrontation.

Attempts at intervention: Loved ones may stage interventions or try to help, creating a sense of care and family loyalty.

Acceptance and boundaries: As the character's behavior worsens, the family may need to set boundaries, adding emotional layers to the plot.

Example: This family dynamic allows the author to portray both the struggle of addiction and the complex, often painful ways that families cope, adding realism and emotional resonance.

Part 3: Improving Writing Craft with AI

In this section, we explore how AI can support authors in refining their writing craft, focusing on tools that enhance grammar, editing, style, clarity, and coherence. As AI technology advances, it provides authors with more than just basic spelling and grammar corrections—it offers tools for improving overall writing quality, enabling authors to create polished, impactful prose. Through AI-powered solutions, writers can address common issues, streamline editing, and bring greater stylistic sophistication to their work.

Chapter 6: Grammar and Editing

AI-Powered Grammar Checkers and Proofreaders

AI-powered grammar checkers and proofreaders have revolutionized the editing process, providing authors with tools that do much more than flag simple spelling and punctuation errors. These tools analyze text with context-aware intelligence, addressing common and complex grammatical issues such as subject-verb agreement, tense consistency, punctuation, sentence structure, and readability. By offering suggestions tailored to specific writing contexts, AI grammar tools help authors produce polished, error-free drafts, saving time and enhancing the quality of their work.

1. Advanced Error Detection Beyond Basic Grammar Rules

Traditional grammar checkers often focus on surface-level issues, but AI-powered tools offer advanced capabilities that address a wide range of subtle and complex errors. These tools can identify issues like homophones, misplaced modifiers, or shifts in tone, improving accuracy and readability by catching details that are easy to miss.

Case Study: Homophone Detection in Fiction Writing

In a fantasy novel, a character might have a distinct name with multiple spellings (e.g., "Kara" and "Cara"). An AI-powered grammar checker could detect any unintended inconsistencies, ensuring that the character's name is spelled consistently throughout the manuscript. Similarly, these tools can catch homophone errors, such as "their" versus "there" or "its" versus "it's," which are often overlooked in manual editing.

Example: An author who has written "their" instead of "there" receives a prompt suggesting the correct term, maintaining clarity in the text.

Example: Catching Misplaced Modifiers in Academic Writing

An academic writer might accidentally place modifiers incorrectly, leading to confusing sentences. For example, "Only students with high grades can attend the conference" versus "Students can only attend the conference with high grades." An AI grammar checker could flag this ambiguity and suggest adjustments for clarity.

2. Adapting Feedback to Different Writing Styles and Contexts

One of the unique strengths of AI grammar checkers is their ability to adapt feedback according to the writing style and formality required for a given context. This adaptability makes these tools effective for a range of writing, from business reports and academic papers to blog posts and creative fiction.

Case Study: Adjusting Tone in Business and Academic Writing

An author working on a business report may need a tone that is concise and professional. AI tools can:

Suggest replacements for jargon or overly complex phrasing, simplifying communication.

Identify passive voice and suggest a more active construction to convey authority.

Example: If a business writer uses, "There is a need to establish strategies for sales increase," the AI might suggest, "We need to establish strategies to increase sales," making the statement clearer and more direct.

Example: Enhancing Narrative Flow in Creative Writing

For a creative fiction writer, maintaining a specific narrative style is essential. An AI grammar tool focused on creative writing might:

Flag overuse of passive voice or excessive adverbs, helping the author maintain a more active and engaging narrative.

Highlight repetitive words or phrases, encouraging varied language for a smoother reading experience.

Example: A sentence like "She quickly ran to the door, feeling very excited" might be flagged by an AI tool, which could suggest, "She dashed to the door, excitement coursing through her," creating a more vivid image for the reader.

3. Contextual Error Detection for Nuanced Language Issues

AI grammar checkers excel at recognizing contextual nuances in language that simple rule-based grammar checkers might miss. By learning from diverse language patterns and datasets, these tools can address issues like inconsistent pronoun usage, unclear antecedents, and context-sensitive vocabulary.

Case Study: Ensuring Consistent Pronouns in Complex Narratives

In a novel with multiple perspectives, AI-powered tools can help maintain consistent pronoun usage and clarity. For instance, in a scene with several characters, an AI tool can track who is being referenced with each pronoun, reducing reader confusion.

Example: If an author writes, "John and David went to the store, but he forgot his wallet," the AI tool could clarify who "he" refers to, prompting a rewrite to avoid ambiguity.

Example: Contextual Vocabulary in Academic Research

Academic writing often includes discipline-specific terminology. An AI grammar checker trained on academic sources can suggest alternative terms or caution against informal language. For example:

Suggested Vocabulary: For a psychology paper, instead of "people get scared," an AI tool might suggest "individuals experience fear," aligning with the formal tone of the field.

4. Instantaneous Feedback for Efficient Editing and Revision

AI-powered grammar tools provide instantaneous feedback, allowing authors to quickly identify and correct errors in real time. This feature is particularly beneficial for authors working on longer projects, enabling them to address issues early on and reduce the number of errors carried through subsequent drafts.

Case Study: Streamlining Editing for a Novel Draft

An author writing a 90,000-word manuscript could spend weeks manually editing for grammar alone. By using an AI grammar tool, the author can:

Identify and correct basic grammar issues before moving on to content-focused revisions.

Catch repetitive language and weak sentence structures that detract from the narrative flow.

Example: By quickly addressing these errors, the author can shift their focus to refining the plot and character arcs without worrying about foundational grammar issues.

Example: Real-Time Feedback for Blog Writers

For a blogger publishing frequent content, instantaneous feedback is crucial for efficiency. AI-powered grammar tools provide real-time suggestions on word choice, sentence structure, and readability. This allows bloggers to:

Produce polished drafts more quickly, keeping up with the demands of consistent publishing.

Address potential issues before publication, reducing the need for post-publication corrections.

5. Personalized Feedback Through Language-Learning Algorithms

Some advanced AI grammar tools provide personalized feedback by identifying recurring errors and patterns in an author's writing. By recognizing these patterns, the tool can offer targeted guidance, helping the author improve over time.

Case Study: Helping Non-Native English Speakers Improve Grammar Skills

For authors whose first language is not English, an AI tool can detect habitual errors in areas like article usage, preposition placement, or verb tense. The tool might provide additional prompts explaining the rule and suggest rewrites to reinforce learning.

Example: If an author consistently misuses articles, writing "He went to library," the AI tool could explain the correct usage of articles in English, helping the writer internalize the rule.

Example: Improving Specific Skills for Academic Writers

An academic writer might struggle with comma placement in complex sentences. An AI tool could flag incorrect punctuation and provide examples of correct usage, helping the author gain confidence with punctuation in future drafts.

6. Enhanced Contextual Understanding for Genre-Specific Writing

Many AI grammar tools are trained on vast datasets, enabling them to recognize language nuances across various genres and writing forms. This understanding allows them to provide genre-specific feedback that respects each form's unique conventions, enhancing both clarity and authenticity.

Case Study: Respecting the Voice in Fictional Dialogue

Fictional dialogue often intentionally breaks grammar rules to convey character voice or dialect. A genre-sensitive AI grammar tool might detect dialogue and adjust its feedback, flagging only errors that hinder clarity rather than stylistic choices.

Example: If a character in a novel says, "Ain't nothing gonna stop me now," the AI tool recognizes the informal tone and avoids suggesting "proper" grammar corrections that would disrupt the character's authentic voice.

Example: Academic Writing Conventions in Scientific Papers

In academic writing, particularly in scientific papers, passive voice is often acceptable. An AI tool could adapt its feedback by flagging passive constructions only if they weaken clarity, rather than universally suggesting active voice.

7. Supporting Higher-Level Revision and Creativity

By taking care of foundational grammar and style issues, AI grammar tools free up authors to focus on more complex revisions, such as plot refinement, character development, and thematic depth. Authors can approach their work with confidence, knowing the basic mechanics are polished and consistent.

Case Study: Supporting Novelists in Plot and Theme Development

For a novelist, eliminating the distraction of grammatical errors enables them to concentrate on deepening the story's themes and refining characters' arcs. Knowing their language is clear and accurate, they can focus on the creative aspects of storytelling.

Example: A novelist working on a complex character-driven story can use AI grammar tools to polish the narrative's language, enabling them to focus fully on intricate character motivations without worrying about sentence-level grammar.

Example: Boosting Creativity for Poetry and Experimental Prose

For poets or authors working on experimental prose, an AI tool can help ensure that creative choices don't inadvertently confuse readers due to mechanical errors. By verifying intentional grammatical decisions, AI allows authors to push boundaries without compromising clarity.

Beyond Grammar: Style and Clarity

While traditional grammar checkers focus on fixing basic errors, AI-powered editing tools go beyond simple corrections to enhance an author's writing style, clarity, and overall readability. By addressing sentence structure, word choice, paragraph organization, pacing, and flow, these tools help authors craft prose that is not only error-free but also engaging, concise, and easy to read. For long-form projects, AI's ability to maintain consistency in style and tone across an entire manuscript is invaluable, enabling authors to polish their work and connect with readers more effectively.

1. Refining Sentence Structure for Improved Clarity

AI editing tools excel at evaluating sentence structure, identifying sentences that may be overly complex, convoluted, or awkwardly phrased. By offering suggestions to simplify or restructure these sentences, AI helps authors make their ideas more accessible to readers.

Case Study: Simplifying Technical Explanations in a Non-Fiction Book

Consider an author writing a non-fiction book on climate science for a general audience. Complex sentences filled with scientific jargon might overwhelm readers unfamiliar with the subject. An AI editing tool could:

Break down complex sentences into shorter, more digestible segments, making the information easier to understand.

Suggest substitutions for technical terms that are accessible to a broader audience, improving comprehension.

Example: A sentence like, "The increased levels of atmospheric CO_2 have precipitated notable perturbations in global weather patterns, leading to intensified meteorological phenomena," might be rephrased by the AI to, "Higher CO_2 levels have disrupted global weather, causing more intense storms and heatwaves." This revision makes the content more engaging and understandable without losing its meaning.

Example: Improving Readability in a Mystery Novel

For a mystery novelist who wants to keep readers on edge, a complex sentence structure might slow down the pacing in a suspenseful scene. The AI tool could suggest breaking long sentences into shorter ones, creating a rhythm that matches the tension of the scene.

Example Revision: The sentence, "As the night deepened, shadows stretched across the room, and every small sound seemed amplified, filling her with a gnawing sense of dread," might be split into, "Night deepened. Shadows stretched across the room. Every small sound was amplified, filling her with a gnawing dread." This revised structure builds tension and draws readers into the scene.

2. Enhancing Word Choice for Precision and Tone

ARTIFICIAL INTELLIGENCE FOR AUTHORS

AI editing tools analyze word usage and choice, helping authors select language that is precise, clear, and appropriate for the intended tone. This feature is especially valuable for authors who need to avoid ambiguous or overly complex vocabulary, ensuring that readers can fully grasp the message.

Case Study: Avoiding Jargon in Business Writing

In a business context, an author might overuse jargon that obscures meaning. For example, "synergize" or "paradigm shift" could be unclear to readers outside of corporate environments. An AI tool could recommend:

Replacing jargon with simpler, clearer words that convey the same meaning without alienating readers.

Example: The phrase, "We aim to synergize cross-functional teams to optimize productivity" might be revised to, "We aim to bring teams together to improve productivity." This change enhances clarity, making the text more accessible.

Example: Elevating Language in Literary Fiction

For literary fiction, where word choice is key to creating a specific tone or mood, AI tools can suggest more evocative language. An author might describe a character's sadness as "deep sadness," but an AI tool could suggest alternatives like "profound sorrow" or "lingering melancholy" to better capture the emotional depth.

Example Revision: Instead of "She felt a deep sadness as she watched the sunset," an AI might suggest, "A lingering melancholy settled over her as she watched the fading sun." This subtle shift enhances the atmosphere and emotional resonance of the scene.

3. Improving Paragraph Organization and Coherence

AI tools provide feedback on paragraph organization, analyzing the flow of ideas within paragraphs and across sections to maintain logical progression. This is particularly useful for non-fiction authors who need a clear, logical structure or fiction authors who want seamless transitions between scenes.

Case Study: Strengthening Argument Flow in an Academic Paper

An academic author may struggle with organizing dense content, such as a thesis or research paper. AI tools can:

Detect topic shifts within paragraphs and suggest reorganization for a more logical flow.

Recommend transitional phrases that bridge ideas, enhancing coherence and readability.

Example: In a paragraph discussing various theories, the AI might detect a sudden shift to a new concept without a transition. The tool could suggest adding a sentence like, "Building on this framework, we now examine alternative theories," to maintain flow.

Example: Organizing Scenes in a Historical Novel

For a historical novelist, AI could help ensure seamless transitions between time periods or locations. If a chapter moves abruptly from one character's perspective to another, the AI might suggest ways to bridge the change:

Adding transition sentences that provide contextual cues, such as "Meanwhile, across the Atlantic, the revolution stirred another group into action," creating a smoother shift for the reader.

4. Adjusting Pacing and Flow for Reader Engagement

Pacing is essential in both fiction and non-fiction. AI tools can analyze factors like sentence length, rhythm, and variation, helping authors adjust pacing to fit the tone of each section. This capability is particularly useful in novels, where different scenes require different paces to sustain reader interest.

Case Study: Maintaining Momentum in an Action Scene

In a thriller novel, an action scene might benefit from short, punchy sentences to convey urgency. If the author uses too many long sentences, the AI might suggest restructuring for a faster rhythm:

Example Revision: Instead of, "She looked around the room, trying to find an escape route while her heart pounded in her chest," the AI could suggest, "She scanned the room. No escape. Her heart pounded." This tighter structure amplifies the tension, keeping readers on edge.

Example: Slowing Down in a Reflective Passage

In contrast, a reflective scene in literary fiction might call for longer, flowing sentences that mirror the character's introspection. If the AI detects too many short, abrupt sentences, it could recommend more complex structures to slow the pacing and allow readers to linger on the character's thoughts.

Example Revision: Short sentences like "He thought about the past. His mistakes haunted him." could be rephrased as, "Lost in thought, he drifted through memories of past mistakes, each one surfacing with a painful clarity." This structure allows the reader to linger on the character's emotions.

5. Improving Readability and Conciseness

Readability is essential for engaging readers, especially in genres that require clarity, such as self-help, non-fiction, or technical writing. AI editing tools evaluate readability scores and suggest rephrasing or trimming overly verbose passages to make content more accessible.

Case Study: Simplifying Language for a Broader Audience in Self-Help Writing

A self-help author may need to reach a diverse audience, making readability critical. AI tools can:

Identify overly complex vocabulary or long sentences that could be broken down to improve accessibility.

Provide readability scores that indicate if a passage is too dense or difficult to follow.

Example: If an author writes, "The manifestation of personal empowerment is facilitated by self-awareness and intentional action," the AI might simplify it to, "Personal empowerment comes from self-awareness and taking deliberate action." This makes the message clearer and more impactful.

Example: Cutting Redundancies in a Blog Post

For a blogger aiming to keep posts concise, AI tools can flag repetitive phrases and unnecessary words. A sentence like "Due to the fact that we are currently experiencing a pandemic, people have become more health-conscious" might be reduced to, "During the pandemic, people have become more health-conscious."

Benefit: This streamlined approach enhances readability, keeping readers engaged without unnecessary detail.

6. Maintaining Consistency Across Long Manuscripts

For authors working on book-length projects, maintaining a consistent tone, style, and level of readability across hundreds of pages is challenging. AI editing tools can track these elements throughout the manuscript, providing feedback that helps authors ensure coherence.

Case Study: Consistent Narrative Voice in a Novel

A novelist may struggle to maintain a consistent tone or narrative voice. An AI editing tool could:

Track stylistic elements like word choice, sentence structure, and tone across chapters, alerting the author to shifts that could disrupt the reader's experience.

Provide feedback on character dialogue, ensuring that each character's speech remains consistent with their personality.

Example: If a character's dialogue shifts from formal to overly casual without reason, the AI might flag this inconsistency, prompting the author to revise for authenticity.

Example: Ensuring Clarity in Technical Documentation

A technical writer developing a user manual needs consistency in terminology, tone, and formatting. An AI tool can help by:

Standardizing terminology throughout the document, ensuring that terms are used consistently and readers are not confused by synonyms.

Highlighting shifts in formality that may occur inadvertently, especially when sections are written at different times.

7. Guiding Higher-Level Revisions in Style and Flow

By handling the foundational aspects of style and clarity, AI editing tools free authors to focus on higher-level revisions, such as plot structure, theme development, and character arcs. Authors can approach these creative aspects with confidence, knowing that the foundational mechanics are sound.

Case Study: Supporting Theme Development in a Literary Novel

An author working on a novel with complex themes may struggle to keep their prose clear while conveying deeper messages. AI tools can:

Flag overly verbose passages where the theme is obscured by dense language, suggesting ways to make the text more accessible without losing thematic depth.

Example: Instead of, "The protagonist's journey was one of self-discovery, culminating in an epiphany that redefined their perception of self and others," the AI could suggest, "The protagonist's journey led to a life-changing epiphany." This clearer, more concise phrasing keeps the theme intact.

Using AI to Improve Writing Style and Coherence

AI-powered tools have become invaluable for authors who want to refine their writing style and enhance the coherence of their work. These tools go beyond error correction, analyzing elements like language usage, tone, rhythm, and structure to help authors polish their voice and ensure their writing flows smoothly. This is especially beneficial for long-form projects, where maintaining consistency in style and clarity can be challenging. With AI's support, authors can create prose that is clear, engaging, and consistent, drawing readers into the story or argument from beginning to end.

1. Identifying Patterns and Enhancing Vocabulary Variety

AI editing tools can detect patterns and tendencies in an author's writing, such as the overuse of certain words, phrases, or sentence structures. This insight helps authors avoid repetitive language, making their prose more dynamic and engaging.

Case Study: Avoiding Overused Words in Fiction Writing

A fiction author may unintentionally rely on certain words like "suddenly," "very," or "just," which can weaken the impact of their prose. An AI tool might flag these repetitive words and suggest alternatives that enhance clarity and tone.

Example: Instead of writing, "She suddenly realized she was very tired," the AI could suggest, "She realized she was exhausted," which is more concise and impactful.

Example in Dialogue: If an author overuses "very" in dialogue to convey emphasis, the AI might suggest replacing it with more descriptive language to enhance emotional impact. For example, changing "I'm very upset" to "I'm furious" adds intensity and precision.

Example: Varying Descriptions in Nature Writing

An author writing a novel with many outdoor scenes might frequently describe trees or sky in similar terms. The AI could flag repetitive phrases like "towering trees" or "blue sky" and suggest alternative descriptions, such as "ancient pines" or "crystal-clear sky." These variations enrich the setting and prevent reader fatigue.

2. Ensuring Tone Consistency Across the Manuscript

Maintaining a consistent tone is essential for an immersive reading experience. Sudden shifts in formality, mood, or style can be jarring for readers, pulling them out of the narrative. AI tools can detect inconsistencies in tone, helping authors ensure that their writing aligns with the intended voice throughout.

Case Study: Maintaining a Relatable Voice in Personal Essays

A writer working on a collection of personal essays may vary in tone from reflective to humorous. However, if a single essay shifts from conversational to overly formal, the AI might flag this inconsistency.

Example: In a humorous personal essay, the sentence, "The experience was intensely enjoyable and led to numerous benefits," could be revised to, "It was a blast, and I gained a ton from it." This informal phrasing aligns with a more conversational tone, ensuring coherence across the essay.

Example: Maintaining Authority in Professional Writing

In business or academic writing, an authoritative tone is crucial. An AI tool might flag a sentence that becomes overly casual, helping the author maintain a professional voice.

Example: "You'll get a lot out of this strategy" could be revised to "This strategy offers substantial benefits." This ensures that the tone remains formal and credible, suited to a professional audience.

3. Enhancing Rhythm and Sentence Structure for Engagement

AI tools can also help authors create varied sentence structures and lengths, adjusting rhythm to improve readability and sustain reader interest. For fiction, this means controlling narrative pace and tension, while for non-fiction, it ensures clarity and flow.

Case Study: Managing Pacing in a Thriller Novel

In an action-packed thriller, an author may want to create a fast-paced rhythm in intense scenes. If the author uses long sentences during these moments, the AI could suggest breaking them up to increase urgency.

Example Revision: "She sprinted through the forest, branches snapping underfoot, heart pounding as shadows flickered around her." The AI might suggest, "She sprinted through the forest. Branches snapped underfoot. Her heart pounded as shadows flickered around her." This revised structure adds tension and speed.

Example: Creating Flow in a Reflective Memoir

In contrast, a memoir might benefit from a slower, reflective pace. If the writing feels too choppy due to short sentences, the AI might suggest merging ideas for a more fluid experience.

Example Revision: "I looked back on those days. They were some of the hardest I'd known." The AI could suggest, "Looking back, I realized those days had been some of the hardest I'd known." This revised phrasing smooths the flow, enhancing the reflective tone.

4. Tailoring Style for Genre-Specific Expectations

AI tools can provide genre-specific feedback to help authors align their writing style with reader expectations. This feature enables authors to adapt their style to fit the conventions of different genres, ensuring that the tone, language, and rhythm resonate with their target audience.

Case Study: Enhancing Descriptive Language in a Romance Novel

A romance novel benefits from vivid, emotional descriptions that draw readers into the characters' experiences. An AI tool designed for fiction might suggest language that conveys a more intimate tone.

Example: Instead of, "He looked at her with interest," the AI might suggest, "His gaze lingered on her, a warm curiosity sparking in his eyes." This phrasing adds emotional depth, aligning with the expectations of romance readers.

Example: Maintaining Precision in Technical Writing

In technical writing, clarity and precision are paramount. An AI tool could identify ambiguous or overly descriptive phrases, recommending simpler language.

Example: A sentence like "The device facilitates high-efficiency operations under a wide range of conditions" might be revised to "The device operates efficiently across various conditions." This phrasing prioritizes clarity, adhering to technical writing standards.

5. Improving Coherence with Logical Flow and Structure

AI tools assist authors in maintaining logical flow and coherence, which is crucial for non-fiction works, complex narratives, or books with multiple subplots. By analyzing paragraph structure and transitions, AI tools ensure that ideas or plot points build naturally, guiding readers seamlessly from one concept or scene to the next.

Case Study: Enhancing Structure in a Non-Fiction Book on Psychology

An author writing about psychology may include multiple sections on theories, applications, and case studies. AI can help identify areas where a topic shift lacks a smooth transition.

Example Suggestion: If a paragraph ends on a specific psychological theory and the next paragraph shifts abruptly to an unrelated case study, the AI might suggest a transition such as, "This theory finds application in real-world scenarios, as shown in the following case study." This ensures readers can follow the argument's progression.

Example: Maintaining Coherence in a Fantasy Novel with Multiple Subplots

In a fantasy novel, an AI tool could help manage transitions between subplots by detecting abrupt shifts in point-of-view characters or settings. If the transition is too sudden, the AI might recommend a contextual sentence to orient the reader.

Example Suggestion: Instead of moving directly from one character's storyline to another's without explanation, the AI might recommend a brief bridging sentence, such as, "Meanwhile, in the kingdom to the east…" This keeps readers grounded in the story.

6. Streamlining Revisions with Personalized Feedback on Style

AI tools can offer personalized feedback on style, tracking an author's tendencies over time and providing suggestions tailored to their unique voice. This guidance allows authors to polish their style while maintaining their individuality.

Case Study: Developing a Stronger Voice for Emerging Authors

For a new author trying to find their style, AI tools might identify habits like over-reliance on passive voice or adverbs, suggesting more assertive language.

Example Suggestion: If an author frequently writes, "The book was placed on the table gently," the AI might suggest, "She set the book on the table with care," enhancing clarity and voice.

Example: Tailored Feedback for Poets

For poets, maintaining a unique voice is essential. AI tools can suggest more precise word choices or flag inconsistent rhythms without altering the writer's personal style.

Example Suggestion: If a poet uses a word that feels out of place within a poem's rhythm, the AI might suggest synonyms that preserve both meaning and flow, helping the poet refine their craft.

7. Enhancing Readability and Audience Engagement

AI tools evaluate readability scores and conciseness, flagging sections where language could be simplified or where sentences could be trimmed to keep readers engaged. This feedback is valuable across all genres, ensuring that readers remain immersed without being distracted by overly dense or verbose passages.

Case Study: Simplifying Language in a Self-Help Book

In a self-help book meant for a broad audience, AI tools could suggest ways to streamline the language, ensuring accessibility for all readers.

Example Suggestion: Instead of, "This approach enables individuals to engage in self-reflective practices that facilitate personal growth," the AI might suggest, "This approach helps people reflect and grow." This revised phrasing makes the message more direct and accessible.

Example: Condensing Academic Writing for Clarity

For an academic paper, AI could flag lengthy, complex sentences, suggesting ways to condense ideas without sacrificing detail.

Example Revision: A sentence like, "The methodology utilized in this study was carefully designed to account for various influencing factors that could potentially skew results" might be revised to, "The study's methodology accounted for factors that could skew results." This streamlined version is more readable and retains essential information.

Chapter 7: Storytelling and Plot Development

In this chapter, we examine how AI can assist authors in the essential tasks of plotting, structuring, and refining their narratives. Effective storytelling relies on a cohesive plot, well-paced story arcs, and consistency throughout the manuscript, and AI-powered tools offer invaluable support in these areas. By using AI to assist with plot outlining, analyze story arcs, and identify inconsistencies or plot holes, authors can strengthen their narrative structure, resulting in more engaging and polished stories.

AI-Assisted Plot Outlining and Structuring

Creating a compelling plot outline is a crucial step in the storytelling process, as it provides the roadmap for key events, character arcs, and central conflicts, guiding the narrative from beginning to end. AI-assisted plot outlining tools support authors by helping them develop clear, structured outlines that ensure focus, consistency, and direction throughout the story. By leveraging AI's ability to analyze story structure and genre conventions, authors can craft engaging narratives that resonate with readers and avoid common pitfalls like pacing issues or plot inconsistencies.

1. Generating Genre-Specific Plot Suggestions

One of the most valuable functions of AI-assisted outlining tools is their capability to generate plot suggestions based on genre norms and story prompts. Drawing from vast databases of successful stories, these tools can provide ideas that align with genre expectations, helping authors structure their stories in ways that appeal to readers.

Case Study: Plot Suggestions for a Mystery Novel

An author writing a mystery novel could input a brief concept, like a detective's journey to solve a decades-old murder. The AI tool can then generate genre-specific plot points, including:

Inciting Incident: The detective stumbles upon a new piece of evidence connected to the cold case.

Rising Action: The detective faces obstacles, including uncooperative witnesses and hidden clues.

Climax: A high-stakes confrontation with the antagonist where the truth is revealed.

Resolution: The case is solved, but lingering consequences affect the detective's life.

Example: By suggesting these core plot points, the AI helps the author establish a framework that aligns with mystery genre conventions, ensuring a satisfying progression that builds suspense and leads to a logical resolution.

Example: Crafting Plot Points for a Romance Story

In a romance novel, AI tools might recommend genre-specific milestones such as the "meet-cute", the first date, misunderstandings or obstacles, the moment of realization, and the reconciliation. These suggestions provide a guide for crafting a romance that meets reader expectations while allowing space for unique twists.

2. Developing Customized Plot Outlines with Character and Theme Integration

Beyond generic plot structures, AI tools can analyze initial story ideas, character motivations, and themes to develop customized plot outlines. By tailoring plot points to align with the author's intended themes and character arcs, AI tools help deepen the narrative and reinforce emotional impact.

Case Study: Building Character-Driven Arcs in a Drama

ARTIFICIAL INTELLIGENCE FOR AUTHORS

An author might input information about a protagonist struggling with loyalty versus ambition. Based on this, the AI tool could generate plot points that showcase these conflicts:

Early Decisions: The protagonist makes a self-serving choice that brings immediate success but strains relationships.

Catalyst for Change: The protagonist's ambition leads to a significant moral dilemma, highlighting the cost of their choices.

Moment of Reflection: The character reflects on the impact of their ambition on loved ones, sparking an internal struggle.

Resolution: The protagonist makes a final decision that reflects their growth, possibly sacrificing ambition for loyalty.

Example: With these plot points, the author can structure events that reveal character development, ensuring the narrative's emotional depth remains consistent and impactful.

Example: Reinforcing Themes in a Science Fiction Novel

For a science fiction novel exploring themes of technology versus humanity, AI tools could suggest plot events that challenge the protagonist's beliefs, such as encounters with AI entities, ethical dilemmas in technology use, and moments where human connection triumphs over mechanical solutions. These thematic touchpoints ensure that the story remains focused and cohesive.

3. Logical Sequencing of Plot Points for Smooth Progression

AI tools can also assist authors in creating a logical sequence of events, ensuring that each plot point builds smoothly toward the next and maintains story momentum. This sequencing is essential in genres like thrillers and dramas, where tension and pacing drive reader engagement.

Case Study: Building Suspense in a Thriller

In a thriller novel, an author may want a major twist to feel surprising yet believable. An AI tool can help by recommending foreshadowing elements in earlier scenes, such as subtle clues or character behaviors that hint at the twist without revealing it outright.

Example of Sequencing: If a plot twist reveals that a close friend is actually the antagonist, the AI might suggest early scenes where the friend displays ambiguous behaviors, like appearing overly curious about the protagonist's secrets or subtly manipulating situations. These moments build a trail of clues that make the twist both shocking and plausible.

Example: Ensuring Smooth Transitions in a Fantasy Epic

For a fantasy epic with multiple plotlines, AI tools can help ensure that plot points transition smoothly. If the story suddenly shifts from one kingdom's conflict to another's, the AI might suggest brief linking scenes or dialogue that bridge these changes.

Example Suggestion: Between major plot points, the AI could recommend a scene where the protagonist receives news of the other kingdom's plight, creating a natural transition and preventing abrupt narrative jumps.

4. Managing Complex Storylines and Interwoven Subplots

For authors tackling complex narratives with multiple subplots, AI tools are invaluable in managing these story layers. They can suggest ways to weave subplots into the main narrative, ensuring that each subplot complements rather than distracts from the central story.

Case Study: Balancing a Romance Subplot in a Sci-Fi Adventure

In a science fiction novel with a romantic subplot, the AI might suggest strategically timed scenes that interweave the romance with the main plot. For example:

Introducing Romance Early: A romantic interest is introduced during a mission briefing, creating initial chemistry within the main action.

Developing During Challenges: The romance develops as the characters face challenges, such as risking their lives together in a rescue mission.

Resolving in Climax: The AI could recommend that the romantic tension reaches a peak during the climactic mission, with the characters' survival depending on their trust in each other.

Example: By balancing the romance alongside the main sci-fi plot, the AI ensures the subplot adds emotional depth without detracting from the primary action.

Example: Reintroducing a Political Subplot in a Fantasy Novel

In a fantasy story with political intrigue, the AI could suggest reintroducing the subplot at critical moments to heighten tension or influence the protagonist's journey. For instance:

Early Setup: Introduce the political faction's interests as a potential threat.

Midway Escalation: A surprising event causes political factions to clash, affecting the protagonist's mission.

Resolution Impact: The protagonist must navigate the political landscape to achieve their goals, tying the subplot directly into the main plot.

Example: This approach creates a sense of interconnectedness, ensuring that subplots support the primary narrative arc.

5. Utilizing Story Templates like the Three-Act Structure and Hero's Journey

Many AI-assisted outlining tools include story structure templates like the three-act structure or the hero's journey. These frameworks offer a classic yet adaptable foundation for authors, guiding them through traditional narrative arcs in a customizable format.

Case Study: Structuring a Fantasy Novel with the Hero's Journey

An author creating a fantasy epic might use an AI tool's hero's journey template, which typically includes stages like the call to adventure, trials, and the return home.

Call to Adventure: The protagonist leaves their ordinary world, driven by a need to save their village from a curse.

Trials and Challenges: The AI suggests encounters with magical beings, betrayals, and internal doubts that challenge the protagonist's resolve.

Return Home: After defeating the antagonist, the protagonist returns, forever changed, to their village.

Example: By following this template, the AI helps the author create a structured yet personalized story that aligns with the hero's journey structure, making the narrative compelling and familiar.

Example: Structuring a Crime Drama with the Three-Act Structure

In a crime drama, the three-act structure helps create a strong, engaging framework. An AI tool might guide the author through:

Act 1: Introducing the crime, establishing the investigator, and presenting the stakes.

Act 2: Escalating tension with multiple suspects and unexpected clues, leading to a major revelation.

Act 3: The final confrontation and resolution, where the investigator uncovers the truth.

Example: This structure provides a reliable narrative framework that keeps the plot tight and focused, ensuring a satisfying build-up and payoff for the reader.

6. Ensuring Cohesion and Focus from Concept to Completion

AI-assisted outlining tools help authors maintain cohesion across the entire narrative, from the initial concept to the final resolution. By continually assessing plot progression, these tools ensure each event aligns with the overarching story and that no threads are left unresolved.

Case Study: Cohesion in a Novel with Multiple Themes

An author writing a novel about identity and redemption may have multiple thematic layers. AI can help ensure that each plot event reinforces these themes, guiding the author to include scenes where the protagonist faces decisions that impact their sense of self and path to redemption.

Example Suggestion: In an early scene, the protagonist makes a morally ambiguous choice; later, a subplot might show the impact of this choice on another character, creating a thematic echo.

Example: Maintaining Focus in a Non-Fiction Self-Help Book

In a self-help book with multiple techniques for overcoming anxiety, AI can help ensure each chapter builds logically on the previous ones, guiding readers step-by-step. If a chapter introduces an unrelated concept, the AI might suggest revisiting earlier themes or techniques to maintain a cohesive flow.

Example Suggestion: The AI could recommend that each chapter conclude with a summary that connects back to the book's primary goal, reinforcing the overall structure and making the narrative easier to follow.

7. Refining Plot Complexity While Retaining the Author's Unique Vision

AI-assisted plot structuring tools provide actionable insights while allowing authors to maintain their unique creative vision. By providing a framework for plot complexity, character arcs, and theme integration, AI tools ensure that the story remains engaging and well-structured.

Case Study: Balancing Complexity in a Historical Novel

For a historical novel with a complex timeline and multiple perspectives, AI can suggest plot checkpoints that keep the timeline cohesive. By offering reminders to revisit certain characters or events, the AI prevents the story from losing focus.

Example: The AI could suggest specific moments for a secondary character to reappear, adding depth to the main character's story arc and ensuring continuity.

Example: Preserving Creative Voice in a Coming-of-Age Novel

In a coming-of-age story with a unique narrative voice, an AI tool might identify plot elements without imposing rigid structures, allowing the author's creativity to drive the flow. If the author prefers a non-linear narrative, the AI could support by suggesting alternative storytelling techniques that retain the voice and enhance the reader's experience.

Analyzing Story Arcs and Pacing

AI tools provide writers with an in-depth look at the natural flow of tension, which is essential for creating engaging story arcs. These tools can assess plot progression, comparing the positioning of climactic moments, twists, or revelations with proven pacing frameworks, such as Freytag's Pyramid or the Hero's Journey. By referencing these structures, AI can guide authors to adjust moments of tension and resolution in a way that aligns with audience expectations.

Example: In a mystery novel, AI might detect that the reveal of a suspect's motive comes too early, potentially diminishing suspense for the reader. The AI can suggest restructuring scenes to gradually build intrigue, leading to a more intense and satisfying climax. Conversely, if the AI identifies a prolonged lull between suspenseful scenes, it might recommend adding foreshadowing or small mysteries to keep the reader engaged.

Case Study: Fine-Tuning Pacing in Thriller Novels

In thrillers, pacing is crucial to sustaining suspense. A 2023 case study of a popular author using an AI tool to edit their manuscript found that AI helped increase reader engagement by analyzing scene lengths and recommending cuts or expansions based on pacing needs. For example, the AI identified overly lengthy dialogue in high-tension scenes, which slowed the action's impact. Based on the AI's feedback, the author shortened the dialogue and added brief, descriptive actions to amplify urgency, resulting in higher engagement in test reader responses.

1. AI's Role in Developing Nuanced Character Arcs

AI is especially helpful for stories with complex character growth. It can track shifts in a character's emotions, motivations, and actions, assessing if changes align with the story's progression. This prevents issues where characters may suddenly transform in unrealistic ways or revert to outdated traits without a clear reason.

Example: In a romance novel, the AI might notice that a character's shift from disinterest to affection occurs too quickly, potentially diminishing the emotional impact. It could suggest a few more scenes to build gradual attraction, strengthening the arc's authenticity. This ensures readers find character relationships believable and relatable, enhancing emotional investment.

Case Study: Developing Nuanced Character Arcs

A fantasy author used AI to analyze a secondary character's arc in a hero's journey story. The AI noticed a gap in the character's motivations between their initial reluctance and later willingness to sacrifice for the protagonist. The AI suggested adding a reflective scene, where the character witnesses the hero's bravery, prompting a more believable shift. This subtle enhancement made the character arc resonate better with early readers, who found the character's growth more emotionally satisfying.

2. Balancing Pacing for Genre-Specific Needs

Different genres demand unique pacing rhythms, and AI can help authors adjust to genre expectations. By analyzing language, sentence structure, and scene transitions, AI provides targeted pacing recommendations that enhance genre immersion.

Example: In horror novels, a slow build-up can increase dread, but intense scenes must come at regular intervals to keep readers on edge. An AI tool could suggest increasing sentence length for slower scenes to enhance atmosphere, while shortening sentences in moments of panic to evoke urgency. Meanwhile, in a romance novel, AI might recommend softer, slower pacing for emotional scenes to allow readers to savor interactions.

Case Study: Historical Fiction

An author of historical fiction leveraged AI to balance action and world-building, two elements crucial in the genre. The AI identified that certain sections detailing historical events were slowing the narrative. By condensing these sections and weaving them more seamlessly into character-driven scenes, the author could maintain the richness of the setting without sacrificing the story's momentum, leading to a more engaging reader experience.

3. Enhancing Scene Transitions and Chapter Breaks for Cohesion

Smooth transitions between scenes help readers stay immersed, and AI tools can identify abrupt shifts that might disrupt flow. By evaluating scene endings and transitions, AI can suggest changes to create a more cohesive narrative.

Example: In a mystery novel, an AI tool might recommend that each chapter end with a subtle cliffhanger or hint about the next clue, building anticipation. For a literary novel, the AI might suggest scene-ending reflections that allow readers to linger on themes before moving forward.

Case Study: YA Fantasy Series

In a YA fantasy series, an AI tool flagged scene transitions that were too abrupt during intense action sequences. The AI recommended inserting brief lines of introspection or scenic detail to give readers time to emotionally process each high-stakes event. Test readers of the revised draft reported feeling more engaged and less overwhelmed by the pacing, demonstrating the AI's effectiveness in enhancing narrative cohesion.

Using AI to Identify Plot Holes and Inconsistencies

Maintaining consistency within a story is crucial for preserving credibility and ensuring that readers remain immersed in the narrative. Plot holes, inconsistencies, or logical gaps can disrupt the reader's engagement, leading to confusion or even mistrust in the story's integrity. AI tools provide invaluable support to authors by identifying potential plot holes and inconsistencies that may undermine the narrative, helping them create a cohesive and believable story. This ability is especially beneficial for authors handling complex plots, multiple timelines, or intricate world-building, where even minor discrepancies can detract from the story's quality.

1. Identifying Character-Based Inconsistencies

One of the key functions of AI tools in storytelling is analyzing characters' actions, knowledge, and behaviors across the narrative, ensuring they align with previously established characterizations and motivations. This cross-referencing capability prevents situations where characters act out of character without proper motivation or awareness of events they shouldn't know about.

Example: In a detective novel, if a side character suddenly reveals information about the crime scene without ever having been there, AI can detect this inconsistency and alert the author. The AI might suggest either revising the scene to include a plausible explanation (e.g., the character overheard someone discussing it) or removing the detail entirely. Such corrections maintain the credibility of characters and prevent the reader from being jolted out of the story by implausible actions.

Case Study: Thriller Writing

A thriller writer used AI to help refine a protagonist's motivations in a draft manuscript. Initially, the character exhibited strong resolve but then displayed sudden hesitation in a high-stakes scene without clear reasoning. The AI flagged this behavioral shift, prompting the author to add a subplot where the protagonist's backstory explains the source of this hesitation. This adjustment not only made the character's actions more coherent but also deepened the reader's emotional connection, as they understood the internal struggle shaping the protagonist's decisions.

2. Spotting Timeline and Continuity Issues

AI tools are adept at catching timeline discrepancies, which can easily occur in stories with multiple events, locations, or perspectives. By analyzing temporal markers, scene progression, and character references, AI can detect when elements don't align within the established timeline.

Example: In a romance novel, an AI might identify if two characters mention the "last time they met" as being weeks ago when the narrative timeline suggests it was only days ago. Similarly, in a sci-fi novel with multiple planets, the AI could flag a reference to "nighttime" on a planet where it was last established to be daytime. By identifying these inconsistencies, the AI helps authors maintain a smooth and believable flow.

Case Study: Historical Fiction

A historical fiction author used AI to help verify timeline consistency in a novel spanning multiple decades. The AI identified several inconsistencies in the ages of characters and the dates of significant historical events mentioned throughout the book. Based on the AI's feedback, the author created a detailed timeline for each character, ensuring age-appropriate behavior and references to historical milestones, which enriched the novel's authenticity and immersion for readers.

3. Ensuring Internal Consistency in Complex World-Building

In genres like fantasy and science fiction, where world-building elements such as magical systems, technologies, or political structures are critical, AI can be instrumental in verifying that these details remain consistent. Even minor deviations from established rules can disrupt the reader's immersion and cause confusion about the fictional universe's logic.

Example: In a fantasy novel, an AI might detect if a character suddenly uses magic in a way that contradicts previously established limitations (e.g., casting a spell beyond their power level without a plausible explanation). The AI can suggest either removing this display of magic or incorporating a justification, such as a magical artifact that temporarily boosts the character's abilities. Such refinements help maintain a consistent and believable world structure.

Case Study: Science Fiction Writing

A sci-fi writer working on a space opera used AI to check the novel's intricate technological rules. The AI flagged an inconsistency where a spaceship, initially described as having limited fuel, later completes a lengthy journey without refueling. Recognizing the discrepancy, the author revised the scene to introduce a mid-way refueling station, preserving the story's internal logic. Early readers of the revised draft praised the story's cohesiveness, attributing it to the thoughtful integration of realistic technological limitations.

4. Detecting and Resolving Unresolved Plot Points

AI tools can highlight dangling subplots or unresolved plot points, ensuring that each narrative element is fully developed or intentionally left open for suspenseful reasons. This function helps authors avoid leaving readers with questions that diminish satisfaction with the story's conclusion.

Example: In a murder mystery, if a subplot involves a character stealing an item early in the story, but the item is never referenced again or tied into the main plot, AI might flag this as an unresolved plot point. The author could choose to revisit and integrate the item into the central mystery, or eliminate references to it if it doesn't add value to the story.

Case Study: Political Thrillers

An author writing a political thriller series used AI to scan the manuscript for unresolved plot points before publication. The AI identified a subplot where a key witness was introduced but never appeared in court or affected the main plot. Realizing the character's importance, the author added a scene where the witness's disappearance is central to the plot twist, tying up the loose end and creating additional suspense. Readers responded positively, noting that the witness subplot added depth and tension to the story's climactic moments.

5. Checking Consistency in Multi-Perspective or Non-Linear Narratives

In stories with multiple perspectives or non-linear timelines, AI tools provide critical support by ensuring each viewpoint aligns with others. This is especially important for genres that involve unreliable narrators or storylines that hinge on multiple interpretations of events.

Example: In a novel told from alternating perspectives, AI might detect discrepancies if two characters recall a shared event with contradictory details that aren't deliberate or meaningful to the plot. The AI can alert the author to either synchronize these perspectives or clarify the contradictions as intentional aspects of the characters' differing perceptions.

Case Study: Psychological Thrillers

A psychological thriller author utilized AI to verify the timeline of two narrators recounting the same series of events in different orders. The AI flagged that one character referenced a clue they hadn't yet discovered according to the timeline. By reordering the scenes and adding transitional explanations, the author preserved the suspense and logic of the alternating perspectives, making for a more engaging and cohesive read.

6. Verifying Consistent Character Development

AI tools help track character traits, motivations, and growth, ensuring that characters evolve in ways that feel natural. Sudden or unexplained changes in a character's behavior can disrupt the narrative flow, so AI assists by highlighting areas where additional context or scenes might be needed to show gradual growth.

Example: In a coming-of-age novel, if a character who previously lacked confidence suddenly displays assertiveness without prior development, the AI might flag this abrupt change. The AI could suggest an added scene where the character experiences a turning point, such as facing a minor conflict that empowers them. This ensures the character's development is realistic and emotionally resonant.

Case Study: Literary Fiction

A literary fiction writer used AI to analyze a character's arc of overcoming grief. The AI detected a sudden change in the character's mood that felt inconsistent with their ongoing journey. Based on AI suggestions, the author expanded the narrative to include a reflective scene where the character speaks with a friend, allowing for a smoother, more realistic transition in their healing process. Readers noted that the revised draft captured the nuances of grief with greater depth and relatability.

Chapter 8: Dialogue and Character Voices

In storytelling, dialogue serves as a powerful tool for revealing character traits, advancing the plot, and creating authentic connections between characters. Writing dialogue that feels natural, engaging, and true to each character's voice can be challenging, particularly when balancing multiple personalities and relationships within a narrative. AI-powered tools provide invaluable support in this area, offering authors the ability to generate, refine, and diversify dialogue. By using AI to generate dialogue options, enhance realism, and develop unique voices for characters, authors can craft more memorable interactions that deepen readers' connections to the story.

AI-Generated Dialogue Options

AI-generated dialogue tools empower authors to create authentic, nuanced conversations that reflect each character's unique personality, relationships, and evolving experiences. By analyzing character traits, emotional context, and relational dynamics, these tools provide dialogue options that align with characters' voices, adding depth and consistency to their interactions. With suggestions tailored to specific situations—such as conflict, high-stakes revelations, or shifting power dynamics—AI allows authors to experiment with tone, pacing, and intention. This flexibility enables writers to craft multidimensional, context-aware dialogue that enriches both character development and story progression, producing a dynamic narrative that resonates with readers.

1. Customizing Dialogue to Character Traits and Speech Patterns

AI dialogue tools offer remarkable specificity, adapting dialogue to match the individual traits and speech patterns of each character. By analyzing character profiles—including details such as assertiveness, humor, formality, or regional dialect—AI can generate lines that authentically reflect each character's unique voice. This attention to detail helps prevent characters from sounding alike, which can happen when authors write multiple voices without fully differentiating them.

Example: Suppose a character in a historical fiction novel is a highly educated, witty aristocrat from 19th-century England, while another is a pragmatic, straightforward sailor. The AI might generate ornate, witty phrasing for the aristocrat, complete with subtle wordplay, while providing blunt, jargon-filled dialogue for the sailor. By presenting these tailored options, AI ensures each character's voice remains distinct, allowing readers to hear their personalities through dialogue alone.

Case Study: Fantasy Dialogue

A fantasy author used an AI dialogue tool to maintain distinct voices among a large ensemble cast. The protagonist, a fiery young rebel, often clashed with her mentor, a wise yet reserved elder. The AI consistently suggested brash, impatient responses for the protagonist and measured, reflective replies for the mentor. This ensured that even in intense scenes, the characters remained authentic. Early readers praised the contrasting voices, commenting that the characters felt vivid and true to themselves.

2. Enhancing Scene Dynamics with Context-Aware Dialogue

AI's ability to analyze the context of each scene—including emotional stakes, tension, and character intentions—allows it to suggest dialogue that fits the scene's tone. This is especially valuable in emotionally complex interactions, where subtle shifts in tone or intent can dramatically alter the scene's impact.

Example: Imagine a scene where two siblings are arguing over a family secret. If the AI detects high tension and lingering bitterness, it might suggest dialogue options that are sharp and direct, conveying anger and frustration. In contrast, if the author seeks a more subdued confrontation, the AI could offer options with gentler phrasing, where each sibling treads carefully. This adaptability lets authors experiment with tone, testing how variations in the dialogue influence the scene's emotional weight.

Case Study: Mystery Dialogue

A mystery writer used an AI tool to develop dialogue in a scene between a detective and a suspect with a tense history. The AI suggested multiple ways for the detective to probe the suspect, ranging from direct accusations to subtle, leading questions. Each approach added a unique layer of tension, with the direct accusation heightening conflict and the subtler option creating an air of suspense. By trying different options, the author discovered a more nuanced path that kept the suspect defensive yet cooperative, which better fit the story's pacing.

3. Conveying Relationship Dynamics through AI-Generated Dialogue

Relationships evolve through dialogue, and AI tools provide options that reflect the changing dynamics between characters—whether it's an escalating rivalry, deepening friendship, or growing romantic tension. By offering dialogue that varies in tone and intent, AI helps authors capture the subtle shifts that mark these relationship developments.

Example: In a romance novel, a scene might feature two characters who are clearly attracted to each other but haven't yet acknowledged it. The AI could suggest playful banter with an undertone of flirtation, hinting at the unspoken feelings without being overly direct. As their relationship progresses, the AI might shift to more vulnerable dialogue options, allowing characters to open up gradually, creating a believable romantic progression.

Case Study: Coming of Age Dialogue

In a coming-of-age story, an author used AI to develop interactions between a protagonist and their best friend, who were drifting apart due to a conflict. Early AI suggestions provided dialogue with hints of passive aggression, reflecting unresolved tension. Later, the AI suggested more open, vulnerable exchanges, where each character finally voiced their frustrations. By selecting these options, the author created a powerful, realistic portrayal of a friendship facing strain and eventual reconciliation, resonating with readers who appreciated the authenticity of the relationship arc.

4. Providing Multiple Options for Conflict and Resolution

In scenes of conflict, AI-generated dialogue offers various approaches to confrontation or resolution, enabling authors to explore different emotional tones and power dynamics. This flexibility allows authors to experiment with how characters express anger, defend their actions, or seek forgiveness, making interactions feel multidimensional.

Example: In a family drama, a mother and daughter might be arguing over life choices. The AI could provide options that range from the mother delivering a heartfelt plea to an outright ultimatum. For the daughter, options might include defensive sarcasm, silent resentment, or a direct rebuttal. Each choice shifts the scene's emotional tone, allowing the author to choose a dialogue path that aligns with the characters' personalities and the desired tension level.

Case Study: YA Dialogue

A YA author wrote a confrontation scene between a high school protagonist and their closest friend over a betrayal. The AI offered options for both harsh, accusatory dialogue and restrained disappointment. By experimenting with these suggestions, the author settled on a tone of restrained disappointment, which aligned with the protagonist's reluctance to lose the friendship. Test readers found the interaction realistic and relatable, appreciating the nuanced portrayal of hurt without outright hostility.

5. Supporting High-Intensity Emotional Moments

High-stakes scenes—such as moments of confession, heartbreak, or confrontation—require precise wording to capture the characters' vulnerability. AI-generated dialogue can offer several nuanced options, each revealing different facets of the characters' emotions, allowing authors to shape the intensity and direction of the scene.

Example: In a thriller, a character might confess their involvement in a crime to a close friend. The AI could suggest dialogue options that convey a range of emotions: from guilt and remorse to defensiveness and fear of judgment. These options help the author decide on the best emotional path, adjusting the dialogue to heighten the impact of the confession on the friendship.

Case Study: Romance Dialogue

A romance author used AI-generated dialogue to craft a pivotal breakup scene. The AI presented lines that expressed everything from resentment to reluctant acceptance, helping the author find a tone that balanced sorrow with maturity. The author ultimately selected dialogue that allowed both characters to express their regrets and maintain mutual respect, adding emotional weight to the scene. Early readers commented on the dialogue's authenticity, praising the bittersweet tone that made the breakup feel grounded and poignant.

6. Experimenting with Power Dynamics

AI-generated dialogue provides options that allow authors to experiment with power dynamics within conversations. This capability is particularly useful in mentor-student relationships, rivalries, or authority-based dynamics, where subtle changes in tone can influence the balance of power between characters.

Example: In a political thriller, a junior agent is reprimanded by their superior. The AI might suggest options for the superior's dialogue that range from a stern, authoritative reprimand to a disappointed, almost paternal tone. Each variation alters the power dynamic, giving the author flexibility in shaping the agent's response. The agent's reply could range from contrition to quiet defiance, revealing layers of their relationship.

Case Study: Courtroom Dialogue

In a courtroom drama, an AI-generated dialogue tool helped an author create the interaction between a prosecutor and a witness who is deliberately evasive. The AI suggested dialogue options for the prosecutor that varied in directness, from subtle leading questions to aggressive challenges. The author chose the more aggressive approach, intensifying the pressure on the witness and escalating the courtroom tension. Early readers praised the scene's pacing and the dialogue's ability to convey authority and desperation, noting it as a standout moment.

7. Enabling Adaptive Dialogue Across Plot Points

AI-generated dialogue options also allow authors to adapt dialogue based on key plot developments, ensuring that characters' speech reflects their evolving knowledge, experiences, and relationships. This adaptability is essential for maintaining coherence and authenticity as the story progresses.

Example: In a mystery novel, a detective might initially speak with a suspect in a professional, courteous manner. But as evidence implicates the suspect, the AI could suggest increasingly confrontational or accusatory language, reflecting the detective's mounting suspicion. By adjusting the dialogue to reflect the shifting plot dynamics, the author ensures that character interactions feel responsive and authentic.

Case Study: Dystopian Dialogue

In a dystopian novel, an author used AI to develop dialogue between a protagonist and a former ally who betrays them. Initially, the AI suggested cordial, cooperative lines, but as the betrayal unfolded, it offered options with a colder, more distant tone. The author selected these adaptive suggestions, allowing the dialogue to reflect the tension and mistrust that developed over time. Readers responded positively, highlighting the dialogue's role in heightening the story's emotional stakes.

8. Exploring Character Motivations through Dialogue Variations

AI dialogue tools enable authors to explore different ways characters might express underlying motivations, providing options that range from overt to subtle. This flexibility helps authors reveal or conceal characters' true intentions, adding depth to their interactions.

Example: In a heist novel, a character with a hidden agenda might give advice to a team member. The AI could provide dialogue options that subtly manipulate the team member, hinting at the character's ulterior motives. Alternatively, the AI could suggest more straightforward advice, letting the author decide whether to conceal or reveal the character's true intentions.

Case Study: Mystery Dialogue

A mystery author used AI to develop dialogue between two characters, one of whom was secretly gathering information. The AI suggested lines that subtly guided the conversation toward specific topics without making the intention obvious. This helped the author portray the character as cunning and strategic, with early readers commenting on the dialogue's complexity and the character's intriguing duplicity.

By leveraging AI-generated dialogue options, authors can create multi-layered, contextually rich conversations that deepen character development and enhance scene dynamics. With dialogue tailored to character traits, emotional context, and shifting power dynamics, authors can craft interactions that feel genuine, adaptive, and memorable. This capability allows authors to focus on refining each line to serve both character and story, ultimately producing a more engaging, realistic, and emotionally resonant narrative.

Using AI to Develop Distinct Character Voices

Establishing unique voices for each character is essential to crafting an engaging and immersive story, as distinct dialogue allows readers to easily identify characters and understand their personalities, backgrounds, and motivations. AI tools offer invaluable support to authors by analyzing character traits, backstories, and relational dynamics to generate dialogue that aligns with each character's individuality. By tailoring vocabulary, tone, rhythm, and style to each character, AI helps create authentic, memorable voices that remain consistent throughout the narrative. This capability allows authors to explore complex interactions and emotional arcs, enhancing both character development and reader engagement.

1. Tailoring Dialogue to Character Traits and Personalities

AI dialogue tools start by analyzing each character's specific traits, such as confidence, humor, caution, or introspection. By doing so, these tools provide dialogue options that reflect the character's personality, ensuring the voice remains authentic and consistent. This attention to personality traits also helps readers quickly identify each character's unique presence within the story.

Example: In a suspense thriller, a detective with a sarcastic, cynical edge might receive AI-generated dialogue that includes sharp one-liners or witty retorts, reflecting their skepticism. Meanwhile, the detective's rookie partner, eager to prove themselves, might have dialogue that's more straightforward or eager, with shorter, to-the-point statements. These contrasting styles help establish distinct personalities and highlight the relationship dynamics in each conversation.

Case Study: Romance Character Voices

A historical romance author used AI to maintain character voice consistency across a large cast. For the main character, an independent, adventurous woman, the AI provided confident, expressive dialogue that often included curiosity-driven questions or daring remarks. In contrast, her reserved love interest spoke in shorter, more formal sentences with hints of restraint. By keeping these voices distinct, the author was able to emphasize their contrasting personalities, heightening the tension and chemistry between the characters. Readers appreciated the authentic voices, noting that each character felt "alive and unique."

2. Adding Depth with Linguistic Nuances and Cultural Context

AI tools can enhance each character's voice by suggesting vocabulary, slang, or dialect that aligns with their cultural background, education level, or social environment. This attention to linguistic nuance ensures characters sound true to their roots and experiences, making their voices more believable and memorable.

Example: In a contemporary novel set in the American South, a character who grew up in a rural area might speak in colloquial language and use idioms unique to the region, like "fixin' to" or "y'all." In contrast, a character from an urban, academic background might use more formal language and avoid regional slang. By incorporating these linguistic distinctions, AI helps the author create a diverse cast whose voices feel anchored in their unique backgrounds.

Case Study: Science Fiction Character Voices

A science fiction writer used AI to create distinct voices for characters from different planetary colonies, each with its own dialect and slang. The AI generated vocabulary and phrasing that reflected each colony's cultural traits, such as formal, almost ceremonial language for a character from a planet with a rigid hierarchy, and more relaxed, abbreviated slang for a character from a working-class mining colony. Test readers enjoyed these nuanced details, noting how each character's speech reinforced their cultural identity and made the interplanetary setting feel authentic.

3. Maintaining Consistent Voices Across Complex Narratives

In stories with multiple points of view, or sprawling narratives with recurring characters, maintaining consistent character voices can be a challenge. AI tools can cross-reference previous dialogue to ensure that each character's speech patterns, vocabulary, and tone remain true to their established voice throughout the story.

Example: In a multi-generational family saga, an AI tool could help maintain consistent voices across time as characters age and experience personal growth. For instance, a rebellious teenager's voice might evolve from blunt, informal language in early chapters to more measured, reflective speech as they mature into adulthood. The AI's consistency checks help the author portray this natural progression, enhancing the realism of character development over time.

Case Study: Fantasy Character Voices

A fantasy author used AI to monitor character voices across a lengthy, multi-book series. In one instance, the AI flagged a line of dialogue in the third book where a reserved mentor figure used overly casual language, which felt out of character. The author adjusted the line to match the mentor's usual formal, careful speech, preserving the integrity of the character's voice across the series. Fans of the series commented on how each character's voice stayed consistent, making it easy to reconnect with familiar personalities even across multiple installments.

4. Crafting Unique Speech Patterns and Rhythms

Each character's voice can be further distinguished by unique speech patterns, such as sentence length, rhythm, and punctuation style. AI tools suggest dialogue that reflects these variations, allowing authors to create voices with distinct rhythms that enhance characterization.

Example: An introspective character might speak in long, complex sentences with frequent pauses, reflecting their thoughtful nature. On the other hand, a quick-witted character could have short, rapid-fire lines, with few pauses and a sharp, snappy cadence. These subtle differences create a unique cadence for each character, making conversations feel as if they belong specifically to those characters.

Case Study: Mystery Character Voices

A detective novel author used AI to develop contrasting speech rhythms for two main characters: a meticulous, methodical detective and their impulsive partner. The AI suggested slower, carefully structured sentences for the detective, who would often pause to choose words precisely, while the partner's dialogue featured short, fragmented sentences with interjections. Readers praised the dialogue for feeling true to each character's nature, commenting on how the contrasting rhythms added to the tension and chemistry between the duo.

5. Showing Character Growth Through Voice Evolution

As characters undergo emotional journeys, their speech patterns and language often shift to reflect their development. AI tools can suggest subtle changes in dialogue that match each character's growth arc, allowing authors to reflect their transformation not only through actions but also in how they speak.

Example: In a coming-of-age novel, a character who starts off insecure and shy might have tentative dialogue at first, marked by hesitant phrasing or self-doubt. As the character gains confidence, the AI could suggest more assertive, direct language, with fewer qualifiers or nervous interjections. This shift in dialogue mirrors the character's inner growth, making their development feel organic.

Case Study: Thriller Character Voices

A thriller writer used AI to depict the journey of a protagonist recovering from trauma. At the story's beginning, the AI suggested guarded, defensive dialogue with brief, clipped responses. Gradually, as the protagonist opened up, the AI recommended longer, more expressive sentences. Early readers noted that the character's voice reflected their healing process, praising how the changes in dialogue subtly conveyed resilience and growth without the need for explicit narration.

6. Reflecting Character Relationships Through Adaptive Voices

Characters often adjust their voices based on whom they are speaking to, whether it's a friend, authority figure, or romantic interest. AI can suggest dialogue options that reflect these relational dynamics, allowing authors to capture the nuances of each interaction more effectively.

Example: In a fantasy novel, a young mage might speak respectfully and deferentially to a mentor but use casual, playful language with a sibling. The AI could suggest dialogue that varies in tone and formality, reflecting how the mage's voice adapts in different relational contexts. These distinctions add layers to each interaction, making relationships feel more authentic and complex.

Case Study: Historical Character Voices

In a historical drama, an author used AI to adjust the protagonist's dialogue across various social settings. With peers, the protagonist spoke freely and colloquially, but with nobles, they used more formal, respectful language. The AI provided suitable variations for each context, enhancing the protagonist's adaptability in navigating social hierarchies. Early readers commented that these shifts in language added realism to the story, as the protagonist's voice felt appropriate to each social encounter.

7. Exploring Power Dynamics and Voice in Conflict Scenes

In scenes where characters confront each other or engage in verbal sparring, AI-generated dialogue can capture shifts in power dynamics. By suggesting different ways to phrase challenges, rebukes, or apologies, AI tools help authors shape each character's response to emphasize their position in the conflict.

Example: In a tense negotiation scene, an AI might offer options for a character to assert dominance through confident, clipped statements or adopt a more manipulative approach with subtle, probing questions. Each option creates a different power dynamic, giving the author flexibility in portraying the tension between characters.

Case Study: Political Thriller Character Voices

A political thriller writer used AI to refine dialogue in a confrontation between a government official and a journalist. The AI offered dialogue variations that ranged from direct, authoritarian language for the official to subversive, challenging remarks for the journalist. By balancing these options, the author captured the push-and-pull of power in the scene, adding suspense and tension. Readers found the exchange gripping, noting how each character's voice communicated their position in the conflict.

8. Developing Distinct Voices for Ensemble Casts

In stories with ensemble casts, each character needs a distinct voice to prevent reader confusion. AI tools help authors craft individual voices that remain unique and recognizable, even in scenes with multiple characters interacting.

Example: In a comedic novel about a group of misfit friends, the AI might suggest sarcastic, quick-witted lines for a character with a dry sense of humor, while providing more dramatic, exaggerated dialogue for another character who's emotionally expressive. These distinct voices make it easy for readers to track each character's contributions, even in rapid-fire group exchanges.

Case Study: Distinct Voices

An author writing a dystopian adventure used AI to ensure each member of a diverse group of rebels had a unique voice. The AI helped differentiate characters by tailoring dialogue: the tech-savvy hacker spoke in jargon-laden, fast-paced language; the stoic leader used short, declarative sentences; and the optimistic newcomer spoke with wide-eyed enthusiasm. Readers noted that each character felt distinct and memorable, enhancing their connection to the group as a whole.

Part 4: AI and the Future of Authorship

As AI becomes increasingly integrated into the creative process, authorship is entering a new era that brings both exciting possibilities and important challenges. This section explores the ethical considerations, biases, and collaborative potential of AI in writing. While AI offers unprecedented support for authors in brainstorming, editing, and refining their work, it also raises questions about originality, ethical use, and the balance between human creativity and machine assistance. By examining these aspects, authors can better understand how to navigate the evolving landscape of AI-powered authorship responsibly and effectively.

Chapter 9: Ethical Considerations and Bias

Addressing Biases in AI-Generated Content

Addressing biases in AI-generated content is essential for authors who want to create inclusive and authentic stories. Since AI models are trained on vast datasets that may contain historical stereotypes and societal biases, AI-generated suggestions can sometimes reflect these biases in subtle ways, affecting character portrayals, language, and narrative themes. To counteract this, authors can adopt a critical approach by cross-referencing AI content with additional research, consulting bias-detection tools, and using specific prompts to guide the AI toward more inclusive representations. By combining AI with their own judgment and cultural awareness, authors can create diverse, respectful narratives that avoid reinforcing harmful stereotypes.

1. Recognizing Bias in AI-Generated Content

AI models are trained on extensive datasets collected from various sources, which inevitably carry the biases, cultural norms, and stereotypes of their origins. This results in AI-generated suggestions that may unintentionally reflect these biases, particularly in how different cultures, genders, races, and socioeconomic groups are portrayed.

Example: Suppose an author asks an AI to generate a dialogue for a character who is a "business executive." The AI might default to generating language that is assertive or focused on financial gain, potentially overlooking softer qualities or diverse perspectives executives can have. Moreover, if prompted to generate a "nurturing" character, the AI may unconsciously suggest more feminine language, reflecting traditional gender stereotypes embedded in the training data. Recognizing these subtle influences is crucial, as they can shape character portrayals in unintended ways.

Case Study: Science Fiction

A science fiction writer using AI to develop dialogue for a multicultural team of astronauts noticed that suggestions for the female characters' dialogue leaned towards caution or emotional expression, while the male characters' dialogue was assertive or technically focused. Recognizing this bias, the author rephrased the AI prompts to include specific instructions on personality traits unrelated to gender, resulting in more balanced and varied dialogue options. This approach helped avoid reinforcing gendered stereotypes, producing a narrative that felt fairer and more inclusive.

2. Verifying Cultural Authenticity and Avoiding Stereotypes

AI can struggle with accurately representing voices from non-Western or marginalized backgrounds, especially when trained predominantly on Western media and literature. This challenge makes it essential for authors to cross-check AI-generated content with external, authentic sources to ensure accuracy and inclusivity.

Example: In a historical novel set in East Asia, an AI might generate dialogue that feels formal and uses generic cultural markers, missing subtleties specific to the time, region, or social class. By consulting authentic sources—like literature from that era or insights from cultural experts—the author can adjust the dialogue to better reflect real customs and communication styles, adding a layer of depth and credibility that AI alone might not capture.

Case Study: Verifying Cultural Authenticity

An author writing a contemporary urban fantasy set in multiple cultural communities used AI to generate initial character dialogue. However, the AI's suggestions for the dialogue of certain characters included outdated or stereotypical expressions. By consulting cultural consultants and sensitivity readers, the author revised the AI suggestions to more accurately reflect each character's background, avoiding potential alienation for readers from those communities. Readers praised the story's respectful representation of different cultures, which contributed to a richer and more inclusive narrative.

3. Using Bias-Detection Tools to Identify Stereotypical Language

Some advanced AI tools now incorporate bias-detection features that help flag language or ideas associated with stereotypes, gendered assumptions, or racial biases. These tools prompt authors to reconsider potentially harmful content before it reaches readers, fostering a more inclusive creative process.

Example: An author writing a crime thriller used an AI tool with built-in bias detection to generate character profiles. When the AI suggested a criminal background for a character based solely on their socioeconomic status, the bias-detection feature flagged it. The author chose to reframe the character's backstory, avoiding stereotypical assumptions and crafting a more nuanced portrayal.

Case Study: Detection Tools

A historical fiction author using bias-detection software noticed that certain dialogue options for working-class characters leaned heavily on slang, creating a caricature rather than a nuanced representation. The bias-detection feature highlighted the imbalance, prompting the author to rewrite the dialogue to be more balanced and realistic. Early readers noted that the characters felt more genuine and appreciated the absence of stereotypical portrayals.

4. Guiding AI with Specific Prompts to Minimize Bias

Authors can steer AI away from stereotypical or generic responses by using precise, detailed prompts that focus on specific personality traits, values, and individual experiences rather than demographic labels.

Example: Instead of asking an AI to generate dialogue for a "young Black woman," an author might specify that the character is a "determined, optimistic young woman with a passion for environmental science." This tailored prompt encourages the AI to focus on the character's personality and goals rather than relying on potentially biased assumptions about demographics.

Case Study: Specific Prompts

A fantasy author writing about a character from an indigenous background initially received AI-generated dialogue that relied on stereotypical phrases associated with spirituality. By reframing the prompt to describe the character's personality, interests, and role in the story, the author received more relevant, respectful dialogue suggestions. This approach allowed the author to avoid clichés, and test readers praised the character for feeling well-rounded and authentic.

5. Advocating for Inclusive AI Development and Training

As the creative industry increasingly uses AI tools, there is a growing push toward building models that reflect a broader, more diverse spectrum of language and experiences. Authors, developers, and researchers are working together to ensure AI tools better represent a variety of cultural, social, and individual perspectives.

Example: Some AI developers are now integrating datasets that include works from marginalized writers and sources from non-Western cultures. This approach helps create a more balanced foundation for language generation, improving AI's ability to provide inclusive and respectful content suggestions.

Case Study: AI Development and Training

A publishing house that regularly uses AI-assisted editing tools began working with developers to integrate bias-awareness features into their workflow. By providing feedback on instances of biased language and advocating for expanded training datasets, the publishing house has seen an improvement in the AI's sensitivity to diversity in language, making it a more reliable tool for inclusive storytelling.

6. Combining AI Suggestions with Authorial Judgment and Research

Authors can view AI-generated content as a starting point, layering in their own research, cultural understanding, and narrative intent to create more nuanced and accurate portrayals. This critical approach involves cross-checking AI suggestions with cultural consultants, sensitivity readers, and reliable sources to ensure accuracy and respect.

Example: When writing a story involving a character from a different cultural background, an author might use AI to generate initial dialogue or scene ideas, then refine these suggestions based on research or feedback from individuals familiar with that culture. This process helps bridge the gap between AI-generated ideas and authentic, respectful representation.

Case Study: Combining AI and Authorial Judgment

A YA author used AI to brainstorm dialogue for a character with a disability. After reviewing the AI's suggestions, the author consulted with a sensitivity reader with lived experience of the same disability.

This collaboration allowed the author to adjust dialogue and character behavior to avoid ableist language or assumptions, creating a more sensitive and authentic portrayal. Readers with similar experiences praised the respectful representation, noting that the character felt genuine and relatable.

7. Empowering Authors to Be AI-Ethics Advocates

Authors using AI can play a proactive role in improving AI systems by reporting instances of biased output and requesting updates. This feedback loop between authors and developers helps build more ethical AI tools that better serve diverse creative needs.

Example: An author who encounters stereotypical suggestions for characters from specific backgrounds can report these instances to AI developers. By providing examples and context, authors can help developers identify areas for improvement in training data and prompt response systems.

Case Study: Empowering Authors to Be AI-Ethics Advocates

A group of writers and publishers worked together to compile and report instances of biased language and stereotypical characterizations generated by a popular AI tool. This initiative prompted the developers to update the model, resulting in more inclusive, nuanced responses in future updates. Authors who participated in the feedback process noted improvements in the AI's cultural sensitivity and its ability to offer varied, respectful character portrayals.

By treating AI-generated content as a collaborative tool, using bias-detection features, providing detailed prompts, and drawing on external research, authors can produce creative work that respects and celebrates diversity. This approach helps authors maintain authenticity and depth while using AI responsibly, ensuring that their stories resonate with readers from all backgrounds. Through ongoing collaboration and advocacy, authors contribute to the development of more equitable AI tools that better serve the diversity of human experience and storytelling.

Ethical Implications of AI in Authorship

The rise of AI in authorship brings with it complex ethical considerations around originality, authorship, and the integrity of the creative process. As AI tools take on larger roles in generating ideas, dialogue, and narrative structure, questions about copyright, ownership, and the impact on human creativity become increasingly relevant. By understanding these ethical dimensions, authors can use AI responsibly—embracing it as a tool for inspiration while preserving their creative vision and ensuring transparency. A thoughtful approach to AI allows writers to benefit from its capabilities without compromising the authenticity of their work or the traditional values of authorship.

1. Navigating Copyright and Ownership Issues with AI-Assisted Content

One of the most pressing ethical concerns surrounding AI in creative work is determining who owns the rights to AI-assisted content. Unlike traditional authorship, where the creator is clearly the originator, AI introduces ambiguity, especially when AI contributes significantly to the storyline, character development, or even specific dialogue. Without clear legal guidelines, authors must navigate uncertain terrain to avoid disputes over intellectual property rights.

Example: An author uses an AI tool to help draft plot points for a novel. If the AI suggests a unique storyline or setting that becomes central to the book, there's a question of whether the author can claim exclusive ownership or if the AI developer holds any rights to that idea. Without explicit terms of service regarding ownership, the potential for disputes is high.

Case Study: Copyright and Ownership

A fantasy novelist who used AI to develop world-building elements found that a critical setting in their novel bore similarities to other fictional works due to the AI's dataset, which drew on public domain and modern texts. To protect their work, the author rewrote these elements to create original, distinct settings, ensuring ownership was not in question.

They also included a statement in the publication acknowledging the initial inspiration from AI but clarified that all final content was the author's unique creation. This transparency helped maintain the author's integrity while respecting ethical boundaries around AI-generated content.

2. Preventing Unintentional Plagiarism in AI-Generated Suggestions

Another ethical concern with AI in authorship is the risk of unintentional plagiarism. AI tools are trained on vast datasets of existing literature and content, which can sometimes result in suggestions that mirror or closely resemble existing works, potentially leading to copyright infringement.

Example: An AI may generate dialogue or plot twists similar to those in popular novels or films because it draws on familiar patterns in literature. If an author inadvertently incorporates these suggestions without realizing the resemblance, they may risk accusations of plagiarism or intellectual property infringement.

Case Study: Preventing Plagerism

A romance author using AI-generated dialogue noticed that certain lines closely mirrored famous romantic scenes from classic literature. To ensure originality, the author ran AI suggestions through a plagiarism detection tool and rephrased similar lines, ultimately making the dialogue their own. By closely reviewing the AI's output and transforming it, the author maintained the integrity of their work, demonstrating due diligence in avoiding unintentional plagiarism.

3. Balancing Human Creativity with AI Assistance

The role of human creativity in authorship is foundational, and some fear that AI's increasing presence in the creative process might dilute the unique insights, voice, and personal expression of the author. When AI takes on tasks like character development, dialogue generation, or thematic structuring, it can reduce the author's role to that of a curator rather than a creator, which raises ethical questions about the essence of authorship.

Example: If an author relies heavily on AI to shape character personalities, plot twists, or narrative flow, they may lose the opportunity to experiment or discover unique ideas that emerge from the human creative process. This reliance can shift authorship toward an act of selection rather than original creation.

Case Study: Balancing Human Creativity

A mystery writer found that their AI tool consistently suggested similar plot structures based on existing mystery novels. Concerned that the AI-generated ideas felt formulaic, the author decided to use AI only in the early brainstorming phase and shifted to manual drafting for core story development. This approach preserved the author's creative influence, allowing AI to support rather than dictate the process. The result was a unique story that readers found refreshing, diverging from typical genre tropes.

4. Embracing AI as a Collaborative Tool

Many writers view AI as a collaborative partner, capable of expanding creative possibilities without replacing human intuition and vision. By using AI thoughtfully, authors can treat it as an assistant that provides inspiration, structural support, or alternative perspectives, which can deepen the creative process.

Example: An AI tool might suggest alternative ways to resolve a plot conflict, introduce unusual character traits, or experiment with narrative tone. Authors can then evaluate these suggestions, deciding whether to integrate, adapt, or discard them based on their creative intent.

Case Study: AI Is A Collaborative Tool

A science fiction author used AI to explore various futures for their dystopian world, allowing the AI to suggest potential conflicts and resolutions. This process inspired the author to incorporate a blend of ideas, merging AI suggestions with their own insights. By treating AI as a brainstorming partner rather than a primary creator, the author felt the story remained uniquely theirs while benefiting from AI's unconventional ideas. The author noted this collaboration in the book's acknowledgment section, crediting AI as a "creative consultant," which readers found intriguing and ethically transparent.

5. Maintaining Transparency and Ethical Standards with AI Usage

Transparency is critical to ethical AI use in authorship, as it informs readers of the extent to which AI contributed to the creative process. By openly acknowledging AI's role, authors can address any potential questions about authorship integrity, allowing readers to appreciate the balance between human and machine input.

Example: Authors can include a note in their books stating where AI was used, whether for initial brainstorming, plot development, or editing. This transparency reinforces the author's credibility, especially if they clarify that AI was used as a tool rather than as a source of core content.

Case Study: Transparency and Ethical Standards

An author of a dystopian novel openly included a statement on the book's copyright page, specifying that AI assisted in generating background details and settings but that all main narrative and character development were original. Readers and reviewers responded positively, noting that the disclosure enhanced their appreciation of the author's ethical approach and respect for the creative process. This transparency served as a model for responsible AI use, allowing readers to understand and value the author's role in shaping the story.

6. Supporting Ethical AI Development and Advocating for Responsible AI Practices

As AI becomes a prominent tool in creative industries, there is a growing movement among writers, developers, and researchers to push for ethical AI practices. Authors using AI can play a vital role in shaping these practices by advocating for transparency, ethical guidelines, and diverse, inclusive datasets that reflect a broad spectrum of human experiences.

Example: Authors can provide feedback to AI developers about instances of biased or stereotypical content, encouraging improvements in the diversity of training datasets. By advocating for responsible AI, authors contribute to an environment where AI tools better serve diverse creative needs and reduce unintended harm.

Case Study: Responsible AI Practices

A group of authors collectively submitted feedback to an AI development company, sharing instances of bias and overly formulaic suggestions. Their feedback prompted the company to integrate a bias-detection feature, which now helps flag problematic language or ideas. This collaboration between authors and developers resulted in a tool that is not only more ethical but also better suited to the needs of a diverse range of creators. Authors who participated in the initiative felt they were contributing to a more inclusive future for AI, setting a positive example for ethical AI use in the arts.

7. Balancing Innovation with Creative Integrity

Using AI in authorship calls for careful balance, ensuring that AI serves as a tool to enhance creativity rather than diminishing the authenticity of authorship. By applying a thoughtful approach—such as clearly defining the role of AI, maintaining transparency, and verifying originality—authors can embrace AI responsibly.

Example: When using AI to assist in developing complex plotlines or character arcs, authors can regularly review and modify AI suggestions, infusing them with their own perspective and creative voice. This ensures that AI remains a supplementary tool rather than the primary driver of creative ideas.

Case Study: Balancing Innovation with Creative Integrity

A literary fiction author used AI in the initial brainstorming stage to explore thematic ideas and alternative perspectives on the protagonist's journey. By refining and adapting AI suggestions, the author wove their own unique insights into the work. They included an acknowledgment of AI's influence while emphasizing the human elements at the heart of the story. This approach enabled AI to serve as a creative catalyst without overshadowing the author's personal vision, setting a strong precedent for ethically integrating AI into the writing process.

In conclusion, the ethical use of AI in authorship requires a conscious, balanced approach that respects originality, transparency, and creative integrity. By actively engaging with AI suggestions, crediting AI's contributions, and supporting responsible AI development, authors can integrate AI in ways that enrich rather than dilute their creative work. This thoughtful engagement with AI fosters a harmonious blend of technology and artistry, empowering authors to push creative boundaries while honoring the values of authentic authorship. As AI tools evolve, authors play a critical role in shaping how these tools are ethically employed in storytelling, ensuring that AI remains a respectful partner in the creative journey

The Future of Human-AI Collaboration in Writing and Storytelling

The future of human-AI collaboration in writing and storytelling holds immense potential to enhance the creative process, empowering authors to push boundaries and explore new narrative possibilities. Rather than replacing human authors, AI serves as a supportive partner, assisting with brainstorming, research, editing, and structural tasks. This collaboration allows authors to focus on the unique elements that bring their stories to life—such as character depth, emotional nuance, and thematic resonance. As AI technology becomes more intuitive and adaptable to individual styles, it promises a creative partnership where AI enhances, rather than diminishes, the author's role, paving the way for innovative and enriched storytelling.

1. Enhancing Creativity with AI as a Collaborative Partner

AI's role in writing is not to replace authors but to serve as a tool that can amplify and support the author's creative instincts. As AI takes on routine tasks—such as research, structural analysis, and editing—authors are freed to focus on elements that infuse a story with originality, emotion, and depth.

Example: A historical fiction author could use AI to quickly gather accurate historical context, names, and events relevant to the story's setting, freeing up time to explore complex character development and plot dynamics. The AI might suggest an event or detail from that period, but the author's role is to shape it within the narrative, using historical accuracy as a springboard for personal, imaginative storytelling.

Case Study: AI as a Collaborative Partner

A screenwriter used AI to organize plot points for a multi-layered, time-travel narrative. While the AI provided structural feedback on pacing and plot coherence, the screenwriter maintained control over character development and thematic depth. The result was a complex, cohesive story that benefitted from AI's organizational assistance while preserving the screenwriter's unique perspective and creative choices. Early viewers noted the clarity of the storyline's structure, a feature enhanced by AI's support.

2. Personalized AI Assistance to Support Unique Writing Styles

As AI continues to advance, future tools will be able to adapt to an author's individual writing style, recognizing and reinforcing their unique voice. Rather than providing generic suggestions, AI could offer input that complements the author's distinct tone, diction, and narrative techniques, making the collaboration feel like an intuitive, personalized partnership.

Example: An author known for lyrical, poetic prose might work with an AI tool that suggests metaphoric language or sensory details, aligning with the author's natural style. In contrast, a thriller writer might use an AI that highlights pacing adjustments to intensify suspense, offering concise, punchy dialogue suggestions that enhance tension without diluting the writer's voice.

Case Study: Personalizing AI Assistance

A mystery novelist with a highly distinctive, minimalist style experimented with AI that had been trained to identify concise, suspense-driven language. The AI suggested dialogue and narrative adjustments that aligned with the author's preference for sparse prose. The collaboration resulted in a novel with an atmospheric, intense tone. Early readers noted that the story's tight, fast-paced structure added to its suspenseful impact, showcasing how AI can reinforce rather than overshadow an author's voice.

3. Keeping Authors at the Helm of Storytelling Decisions

A crucial aspect of future human-AI collaboration in writing is maintaining authors as the guiding force behind the creative process. AI may offer ideas, but it's up to the author to select and shape those ideas in ways that serve their story's unique direction, themes, and character arcs. This balance ensures that while AI can contribute to ideation, the human author ultimately decides the path each story takes.

Example: An AI might suggest alternative plot twists or backstory elements for a character, but the author selects the direction that aligns best with the character's arc and thematic focus. This allows AI to provide variety without compromising the author's original vision and narrative control.

Case Study: Keeping Authors at the Helm

A fantasy author used AI to brainstorm potential endings for an epic novel. The AI suggested a variety of resolutions, from triumphant to tragic, but the author chose an ending that reflected the book's central theme of resilience. By combining AI's ideas with their vision, the author created an ending that resonated with readers as both unexpected and deeply satisfying, demonstrating that AI can enrich creative options without diminishing the author's role.

4. Expanding Storytelling Boundaries with AI-Driven Innovation

AI has the potential to support authors in exploring new storytelling formats, such as interactive narratives, augmented reality, and multimedia storytelling. By helping authors manage complex structures, character interactions, and multi-layered plots, AI can make ambitious projects more accessible and allow writers to push traditional storytelling boundaries.

Example: An author creating a choose-your-own-adventure book could use AI to analyze the impact of each decision path, ensuring a cohesive and engaging experience regardless of the reader's choices. Similarly, a writer interested in augmented reality storytelling could use AI to suggest interactive elements that align with the story's themes, creating a seamless blend of narrative and technology.

Case Study: Expanding Storytelling Boundaries

A sci-fi writer collaborated with AI to develop an interactive, multi-narrative story where readers could switch between different characters' perspectives. The AI helped manage each storyline's pacing and cross-referenced details to maintain consistency across plotlines. Test readers were impressed with the immersive experience, noting that the story felt cohesive and dynamic despite its complexity. This case illustrates how AI can empower authors to experiment with formats that enhance reader engagement.

5. Preserving the Uniquely Human Aspects of Storytelling

While AI can assist with structure, research, and ideation, there are certain qualities of storytelling—such as empathy, emotional intuition, and cultural understanding—that remain uniquely human. The author's role in bringing personal experience, emotional insight, and nuanced perspectives to a story ensures that the resulting work resonates on a deeper level with readers.

Example: AI might suggest a logical progression of events for a character arc, but the author's understanding of human emotions allows them to add layers of vulnerability, internal conflict, or personal growth that AI alone cannot replicate. This human touch imbues characters and narratives with authenticity, reflecting the complexities of real-life experiences and relationships.

Case Study: Uniquely Human Aspects of Storytelling

A memoirist using AI to organize narrative structure found that the tool offered helpful suggestions on pacing and sequencing events. However, the author added personal insights and reflections, deepening the emotional resonance. Readers connected deeply with the memoir, particularly the sections exploring family dynamics and personal resilience, demonstrating how the author's lived experience provided an essential human element AI could not replicate.

6. Encouraging Ethical Use and Transparent Acknowledgment of AI's Role

As human-AI collaboration grows, it's important for authors to remain transparent about AI's involvement in their work. Clear acknowledgment of AI's contributions can foster trust with readers, who may value knowing the degree to which AI assisted in the creative process. Such transparency also allows authors to demonstrate ethical responsibility in their use of technology.

Example: Authors might include a note on the title page or in the acknowledgments, explaining AI's role in supporting tasks such as research, initial brainstorming, or editing. This fosters reader confidence in the integrity of the work and clarifies that AI was used as a supportive tool, not a substitute for the author's creative input.

Case Study: Acknowledgment of AI's Role

A novelist used AI for editing and feedback on pacing but ensured that all plot and character development was done independently. In the book's acknowledgments, the author mentioned AI's role in the editing process, reinforcing their commitment to transparency. Readers appreciated the note, expressing confidence that the story's creative elements were distinctly the author's own, and saw the AI acknowledgment as a respectful nod to the tool's role in enhancing the book's quality.

7. Shaping the Future of Storytelling through Human-AI Collaboration

As AI becomes more integrated into creative industries, authors are uniquely positioned to shape how AI is used responsibly and creatively in storytelling. Through active feedback and collaboration, writers can influence the development of AI tools that support diverse, ethical, and imaginative storytelling.

Example: Authors who encounter biased or formulaic suggestions from AI can provide feedback to developers, advocating for updates that reflect a broader range of perspectives. This feedback loop helps improve AI's sensitivity to diversity and inclusivity, creating tools that are more responsive to the needs of a wide range of authors and stories.

Case Study: Future of Storytelling

A group of authors partnered with an AI development team to create an AI-driven platform that supports inclusive storytelling. The authors provided insights on biases they encountered, and the developers worked to create bias-detection features. The collaboration resulted in an AI tool better suited to producing diverse and ethical creative content, setting a standard for responsible AI in the arts. Authors involved in the project felt empowered, knowing their feedback contributed to a tool that aligned with their values and the needs of diverse storytellers.

Chapter 10: The Author's Role in the AI Age

As AI becomes an integral part of the writing process, authors are entering a new era that both challenges and reshapes traditional notions of authorship. With AI tools assisting in brainstorming, editing, and even suggesting stylistic adjustments, authors are faced with the task of defining their role in an age where technology can assist in every aspect of storytelling. This chapter examines the evolving responsibilities and opportunities for authors, emphasizing the unique contributions that human creativity brings to the art of writing. By adapting to AI's presence, embracing it as a supportive tool, and valuing their own creative instincts, authors can continue to play a central role in the future of literature and storytelling.

Adapting to the Changing Landscape of Authorship

As AI becomes more integrated into the creative process, the role of the author is evolving, presenting new challenges and opportunities in storytelling. While AI tools can streamline tasks like research, editing, and idea generation, authors must decide how to incorporate these technologies in ways that enhance, rather than replace, their unique creative input. By thoughtfully adapting to AI's capabilities, authors can focus on the imaginative and emotional depth of their work, exploring ambitious new formats and genres with AI as a supportive partner. This evolving landscape empowers authors to expand their storytelling possibilities while preserving the authenticity and integrity of their voices.

1. Navigating AI's Expanding Role in the Writing Process

ARTIFICIAL INTELLIGENCE FOR AUTHORS

As AI tools take on an increasing range of tasks, from brainstorming to drafting, authors are faced with choices about how and when to use these technologies in their work. While AI can handle routine tasks with efficiency, authors must decide where they want to maintain personal involvement to preserve the uniqueness of their storytelling.

Example: A historical fiction writer might use AI to gather preliminary research on a particular time period, such as names of real locations or social customs, but then take over to bring these elements to life in ways AI cannot—adding their own interpretation and emotional resonance to scenes. By using AI for specific research tasks, the author maintains control over the narrative's voice and depth.

Case Study: Navigating AI's Expanding Role

A fantasy author experimented with an AI tool to generate character backstories and found the AI's suggestions helpful for outlining the relationships between different factions in their world. However, they soon realized the AI's suggestions lacked the nuance and moral ambiguity they envisioned for their characters. Ultimately, the author decided to use AI-generated ideas as a foundation but to personally revise each backstory to reflect the emotional complexity they wanted, balancing AI efficiency with hands-on creativity.

2. Streamlining the Writing Process with AI

The incorporation of AI allows authors to streamline many stages of the writing process, saving time on research, plotting, and editing so they can focus more on creative development. By alleviating routine tasks, authors can invest more energy in refining their themes, emotional arcs, and character depth.

Example: An author writing a science fiction novel might use AI to suggest technical jargon or futuristic terminology, helping them quickly build an authentic sci-fi setting. With these logistical details handled, the author can focus on exploring philosophical themes or character-driven conflict, enriching the narrative's depth.

Case Study: Streamlining the Writing Process

A romance writer struggling to meet deadlines incorporated an AI tool for initial grammar and spelling checks. This allowed the writer to concentrate on refining the emotional dialogue and intricate dynamics between characters. By handling editing tasks efficiently, AI enabled the writer to focus on crafting dialogue and interactions that resonated with readers. The result was a polished, emotionally impactful story completed in less time, demonstrating AI's value as a productivity tool that enhances the author's creative focus.

3. Exploring New Genres, Styles, and Narrative Structures with AI Assistance

AI can provide authors with structural support and genre insights that encourage them to experiment with new formats and storytelling techniques. By offering suggestions that align with genre conventions or alternative narrative structures, AI enables authors to push creative boundaries and expand their storytelling skills.

Example: An author used to writing realistic fiction might use AI to experiment with speculative fiction. The AI could suggest speculative elements, such as a society governed by surreal laws or futuristic technologies, that inspire the author to explore themes of morality or power in imaginative new ways.

Case Study: Exploring New Genres

A thriller author interested in branching out into non-linear storytelling used an AI tool to help organize multiple timelines. The AI suggested plot points that could be introduced at different intervals to maintain suspense and guide the reader through the complex structure. The author found that AI's suggestions made the non-linear format manageable and engaging, allowing them to experiment successfully with a storytelling technique they'd previously found daunting.

4. Leveraging AI Feedback to Deepen Story Insights

AI's capacity to analyze patterns in writing, such as pacing, dialogue flow, and emotional arcs, offers authors valuable insights to strengthen their work. Rather than replacing human judgment, AI feedback serves as an analytical tool, helping authors pinpoint areas for improvement and refine their narrative's impact.

Example: An AI tool might analyze pacing in a novel and highlight sections where the tension lags or where character development needs reinforcing. The author can then use this feedback to make adjustments that heighten suspense or deepen character relationships, enhancing the story's overall flow and resonance.

Case Study: Deepen Story Insights

A mystery author using AI feedback to refine pacing noticed the tool flagged several scenes as overly detailed, which slowed down the suspense. Based on this analysis, the author revised these sections, trimming unnecessary details and adding moments of tension. Early readers found the revised version more gripping and immersive, illustrating how AI feedback can support authors in enhancing the reading experience without diminishing their creative control.

5. Defining the Author's Role in an AI-Integrated Workflow

As AI becomes an increasingly common part of the writing process, authors must redefine their role, identifying which aspects of their work they want to preserve as uniquely human. This involves deciding which tasks to delegate to AI and which to handle directly, creating a customized workflow that honors their creative vision.

Example: An author may choose to use AI exclusively for initial brainstorming or editing while reserving story development and character dialogue for personal drafting. By drawing these boundaries, the author ensures AI serves a supporting role rather than dictating the creative direction.

Case Study: Author's Role in an AI-Integrated Workflow

A literary fiction author experimenting with AI discovered that while AI-generated plot points could be helpful for brainstorming, the resulting suggestions often lacked the subtlety and emotional nuance they valued in their work. The author chose to use AI only during the editing stage to check grammar and flow, ensuring their storytelling remained rooted in personal insight. This selective use of AI enabled the author to maintain creative authenticity while benefiting from AI's technical assistance.

6. Expanding Storytelling Possibilities with Human-AI Collaboration

The changing landscape of authorship, with AI as a collaborative tool, opens doors for authors to experiment with more ambitious projects and explore storytelling formats that might otherwise feel out of reach. With AI handling logistical elements, authors can dedicate more time and energy to exploring themes, emotions, and complex narratives.

Example: An author interested in writing an immersive, multi-threaded novel might use AI to keep track of the various narrative strands, ensuring each storyline contributes to the overall thematic arc. This allows the author to explore complex ideas without losing control over the story's cohesion.

Case Study: with Human-AI Collaboration

A writer creating an interactive narrative used AI to generate multiple decision points for readers, each impacting the story's direction. The AI helped manage the branching plotlines, maintaining a cohesive storyline regardless of the reader's choices. Test readers praised the interactive experience, and the author noted that AI enabled them to take on a project they wouldn't have attempted alone, highlighting AI's potential to make complex storytelling accessible.

7. Balancing Tradition and Innovation in the Future of Authorship

As authors adapt to AI's expanding role, they face the challenge of balancing traditional storytelling values with new technological possibilities. By thoughtfully integrating AI, authors can preserve the authenticity of their voice while benefiting from AI's efficiencies, creating a future where human insight and technological innovation coexist.

Example: In crafting character arcs, an author might consult AI to suggest potential motivations or backstories, but then shape these ideas through their own understanding of human psychology, ensuring each character feels genuine and layered. AI provides inspiration, but the author's insights and lived experience ultimately guide the character's journey.

Case Study: Balancing Tradition and Innovation

A memoirist used AI to organize a non-linear structure for their life story but chose to write each section independently, imbuing it with personal reflection and emotional depth. While AI provided structural support, the memoir's emotional weight came from the author's personal engagement with each chapter. Readers appreciated the authenticity and clarity, illustrating how AI and human creativity can complement each other when applied thoughtfully.

8. Reimagining Authorship in the Age of Human-AI Collaboration

The evolving landscape of authorship with AI support encourages authors to redefine their roles and adapt their workflows, blending personal creativity with technological efficiency. By maintaining control over core story elements, authors can use AI to expand their creative possibilities without compromising their unique voice.

Example: An author working on a mystery novel could use AI for idea generation and structural suggestions, yet rely on personal intuition to refine character psychology and nuanced dialogue, ensuring the story retains its emotional depth and originality.

Case Study: Reimagining Authorship

A YA fantasy author used AI to manage complex subplots across a trilogy, using the tool to keep each book aligned with the overarching narrative. However, the author took charge of character development, ensuring that each protagonist's journey evolved naturally. This collaboration allowed the author to focus on emotional arcs while benefiting from AI's structural support. Fans praised the series for its consistency and rich character development, showing that AI can enhance storytelling without overshadowing human creativity.

In summary, adapting to AI's presence in authorship offers authors opportunities to redefine and expand their role in storytelling. By thoughtfully integrating AI into their creative processes, authors can enhance their productivity, experiment with new storytelling techniques, and tackle ambitious projects with confidence. This balance allows authors to preserve the authenticity of their voices while benefiting from AI's efficiencies, ushering in a future where human insight and technology work in harmony to enrich the art of storytelling. Through this collaborative approach, authors can continue to tell powerful, resonant stories that honor tradition while embracing innovation.

Embracing AI as a Tool, Not a Replacement

As AI becomes a powerful presence in the creative process, it's essential for authors to embrace it as a supportive tool rather than a replacement for their unique voice and creativity. AI offers valuable assistance in areas like editing, brainstorming, and structural analysis, allowing authors to streamline certain tasks while retaining control over the emotional and thematic heart of their work. By using AI to complement their strengths and enhance productivity, authors can focus on the imaginative and personal elements that make their stories resonate, ensuring that AI serves as a partner rather than a substitute in the storytelling journey.

1. Leveraging AI for Practical Support in the Writing Process

In today's creative landscape, AI offers valuable practical support that allows authors to streamline certain aspects of writing, freeing up more time and mental energy for the core creative work. By using AI to handle tasks such as idea generation, structural analysis, stylistic suggestions, and editing, authors can improve their workflow while ensuring that their personal creativity drives the story.

Example: An author working on a thriller might use AI to generate possible plot twists or alternative directions for a suspenseful scene. Rather than accepting these AI-generated ideas wholesale, the author selects one suggestion and modifies it to fit the story's tone, adding unique elements that resonate with their narrative. This approach allows AI to assist with brainstorming, but the final creative direction remains in the author's hands.

Case Study: Leveraging AI for Practical Support

A fantasy writer faced writer's block when crafting dialogue for a climactic confrontation scene. They turned to an AI tool that offered various tones—ranging from accusatory to sorrowful. After reviewing the options, the author selected a tone that suited the emotional intensity they envisioned and used it as a springboard to write the final dialogue. This collaborative use of AI allowed the author to overcome creative stagnation while ensuring the scene retained its original emotional impact, highlighting AI's role as a supportive tool rather than a creative replacement.

2. Enhancing Efficiency Without Sacrificing Originality

AI can take on mechanical and organizational tasks that might otherwise drain the author's time and focus. By letting AI handle grammar corrections, stylistic suggestions, or data organization, authors can concentrate on the imaginative aspects of storytelling that demand human insight and originality.

Example: An author working on a science fiction novel uses AI for basic grammar and style checks, making it easy to spot typos, overused phrases, or clarity issues. This allows the author to maintain high-quality language without getting bogged down in technical editing, giving them more space to focus on world-building and character development— elements that require human creativity and attention to detail.

Case Study: Efficiency Without Sacrifice

A memoirist used AI to organize and categorize research materials, such as historical timelines and personal anecdotes, which they could refer to throughout the drafting process. By having the logistical tasks managed by AI, the author was able to concentrate on introspective reflection and thematic connections, ultimately creating a deeply personal narrative. Early readers praised the memoir's cohesive storytelling and emotional resonance, showcasing how AI can support efficiency while preserving the author's authentic voice.

3. Using AI to Generate Ideas Without Losing Creative Control

AI's ability to provide suggestions can be a valuable source of inspiration, especially when authors face creative blocks or are exploring new genres or styles. However, these suggestions work best as starting points that the author refines and personalizes, ensuring the final product remains a reflection of their unique creative vision.

Example: A mystery writer might use AI to brainstorm potential suspects and motives in a whodunit plot. While the AI can generate a list of possibilities, the author selects the ideas that align with the story's tone and theme, adding depth and complexity to each character. This way, AI's suggestions serve as an initial framework that the author builds upon, ensuring the plot remains fresh and distinctive.

Case Study: Generate Ideas Without Losing Creativity

A historical romance author interested in incorporating supernatural elements used AI to brainstorm various mythological themes and settings. The AI provided suggestions based on folklore, but the author adjusted these elements to fit the story's romantic and historical context, giving the supernatural aspects a unique twist. The author credited AI as an inspiration tool, noting that its ideas helped expand the story's scope while allowing them to retain full creative control.

4. Maintaining the Unique Emotional and Thematic Depth of the Author's Voice

One of the fundamental limitations of AI is its inability to capture the emotional complexity and thematic depth that define impactful storytelling. While AI can provide structural or stylistic guidance, it cannot replicate the empathy, intuition, and personal insight that authors bring to their work. By recognizing this distinction, authors can ensure that their creative voice remains central.

Example: AI may suggest pacing adjustments for improved flow in a dramatic scene, but only the author can decide which moments need to linger for emotional impact and where subtle shifts in tone can reveal character vulnerabilities. This careful balance ensures that the story's emotional journey remains authentic to the author's vision.

Case Study: Unique Emotional and Thematic Depth

A literary fiction writer used AI to analyze pacing and received suggestions to shorten several reflective passages. However, the author chose to keep these passages as they believed they contributed to the story's meditative tone. This decision, driven by personal insight, ultimately preserved the novel's contemplative atmosphere, demonstrating that AI's role is to support but never dictate artistic choices.

5. Balancing Efficiency and Authenticity

By treating AI as a partner, authors can achieve a balanced approach to writing, where AI handles technicalities, and the author retains control over storytelling elements that require emotional resonance and artistic intuition. This partnership enables authors to produce work that is both technically polished and creatively authentic.

Example: An author drafting a children's book uses AI to check for vocabulary that aligns with the target age group. The AI tool ensures language clarity, while the author focuses on crafting engaging characters and themes that address young readers' experiences and emotions. This division of labor allows AI to enhance readability while preserving the author's role in shaping an impactful story.

Case Study: Balancing Efficiency and Authenticity

A YA fantasy author relied on AI for chapter-by-chapter summaries to streamline editing. By letting AI handle summarization, the author could concentrate on deepening themes of resilience and friendship. Readers praised the book for its powerful themes and engaging plot, illustrating how AI can support narrative cohesion while allowing the author's emotional insight to take center stage.

6. Encouraging a Collaborative Mindset Toward AI

Approaching AI as a collaborative partner rather than a replacement encourages authors to make intentional choices about how to use technology without compromising their unique creative voice. This mindset allows AI to inspire, assist, and expand possibilities while leaving the final creative direction in the author's hands.

Example: An author working on a memoir might use AI to generate questions or prompts based on different periods in their life. These prompts can inspire reflections or memories that enrich the narrative. However, the author decides which stories to tell and how to convey personal experiences, ensuring the memoir remains an authentic reflection of their journey.

Case Study: Collaborative Mindset

A horror author used AI to brainstorm atmospheric descriptions but personalized each scene with sensory details specific to the story's setting. While AI provided general imagery suggestions, the author added descriptions based on personal memories of eerie landscapes. Readers noted the vivid, chilling atmosphere, which felt grounded and realistic, demonstrating how AI can offer general inspiration while the author's personal touches create a lasting impact.

7. Empowering Authors to Preserve the Uniquely Human Aspects of Storytelling

Ultimately, by embracing AI as a supportive tool, authors can preserve the human qualities that make stories meaningful—such as empathy, intuition, and individual perspective. These aspects, irreplaceable by AI, are what enable authors to create narratives that connect with readers on a personal level.

Example: An AI may offer structurally sound suggestions for a story's climax, but the author chooses the emotional peak and resolution based on their understanding of the characters' journeys. This human touch, driven by empathy and personal experience, is essential for an impactful narrative.

Case Study: Empowering Authors

A sci-fi author using AI for background research on space travel found inspiration for world-building but added details inspired by their childhood love of stargazing. The combination of AI-driven research and personal memories gave the story an intimate quality, making the futuristic setting feel authentic. Early readers connected with the novel's blend of science and nostalgia, highlighting how AI can expand possibilities while the author's perspective creates emotional depth.

The Unique Value of Human Creativity and Intuition

While AI can assist with technical aspects of writing, the core of storytelling remains uniquely human, driven by creativity, intuition, and emotional intelligence. Authors bring irreplaceable qualities—such as lived experience, empathy, and an understanding of complex emotions—that AI cannot replicate. These human elements infuse stories with authenticity, cultural relevance, and thematic depth, creating narratives that resonate on a personal level. By embracing AI as a tool to enhance their process rather than replace it, authors can preserve the soul of their work, ensuring that literature continues to reflect the richness of human experience.

1. The Irreplaceable Depth of Human Experience in Storytelling

AI may excel at generating language patterns or suggesting story structures, but it cannot replicate the lived experience that human authors bring to their work. Storytelling is rooted in personal histories, cultural perspectives, and emotional complexity, which enable authors to create narratives that resonate with the authentic highs and lows of life. This depth is why readers connect so profoundly with human-authored stories—because they are infused with empathy, nuance, and understanding that reflect real life.

Example: A memoir writer drawing on personal experiences of grief brings an authenticity to their narrative that AI cannot replicate. AI might analyze patterns in language related to loss or provide structural suggestions, but it cannot know the specific, visceral experience of grief. Only a human author can convey the unpredictability and intensity of such emotions, crafting a narrative that resonates deeply with readers who have shared similar feelings.

Case Study: Human Experience in Storytelling

A war journalist turned novelist used their personal experiences in conflict zones to write a fictional story about resilience in the face of trauma. While AI provided suggestions for pacing and structure, it was the author's intimate understanding of fear, courage, and survival that gave the story its emotional impact. Early readers, including those who had lived through similar situations, found the narrative powerful and authentic, underscoring the irreplaceable role of human experience in creating meaningful literature.

2. Human Creativity: Guided by Intuition, Shaped by Emotion

AI operates on probabilities and patterns, but human intuition allows authors to make choices that are unpredictable yet deeply meaningful. This intuition—an instinctive feel for a story's direction, tone, or thematic depth—leads authors to make narrative decisions that may defy convention but connect profoundly with readers. These creative leaps, driven by an author's "gut feeling," are uniquely human and give stories an originality and depth that AI-generated content lacks.

Example: In the middle of writing a novel, an author might feel compelled to shift a protagonist's arc in an unexpected direction—

perhaps turning a hero into a tragic figure or revealing a vulnerability that was previously hidden. This instinct-driven choice creates layers of complexity that resonate with readers, who see reflections of real human unpredictability and growth.

Case Study: Guided by Intuition, Shaped by Emotion

A fantasy author found themselves intuitively moving toward a more tragic ending than originally planned, sensing that it would create a more impactful narrative. An AI tool had suggested a more conventional "heroic victory," but the author's choice to embrace a bittersweet resolution resonated with readers, who found the ending moving and thought-provoking. This example demonstrates how human intuition often leads to deeper, more nuanced storytelling than AI's pattern-based suggestions.

3. Emotional Intelligence: The Heart of Authentic Storytelling

One of the most significant limitations of AI is its inability to feel emotions or truly understand human relationships. Emotional intelligence—the ability to recognize, understand, and respond to emotions in oneself and others—is essential for creating characters that feel real and for exploring complex interpersonal dynamics. This quality allows authors to build stories that capture the essence of human connections, conflict, and transformation.

Example: When writing a romance, an author brings their understanding of love's complexities—its vulnerability, intensity, and challenges—to craft moments that feel genuine and moving. While AI might suggest dialogue patterns for a romantic interaction, only the author can infuse these interactions with the subtlety and authenticity that reflects real relationships.

Case Study: Emotional Intelligence

A romance novelist exploring themes of forgiveness and personal growth used AI to generate dialogue suggestions but made significant adjustments based on their emotional insight. The author rewrote several scenes to reflect the nuances of reconciliation, making sure each line resonated with the complexities of love and regret. The book's success underscored how human insight into emotions is critical for creating authentic and resonant romance narratives.

4. Cultural Sensitivity and Symbolism: The Layers of Meaning AI Cannot Grasp

Storytelling often carries cultural significance and symbolic meaning, with authors drawing on shared histories, myths, and symbols to enrich their narratives. This sensitivity to culture and symbolism is something AI lacks, as it doesn't have the lived context needed to understand or convey these elements authentically. Human authors, by contrast, can draw on their cultural backgrounds and societal insights to craft stories that reflect shared values, explore relevant themes, and resonate on a communal level.

Example: In writing about a family's journey through generational trauma, an author might incorporate cultural symbols—like a family heirloom or traditional ritual—that evoke themes of resilience and legacy. These symbols carry layers of meaning for readers from similar backgrounds, creating a story that is both personal and universally relatable.

Case Study: Cultural Sensitivity and Symbolism

A Nigerian author writing about cultural identity used AI for preliminary organization of historical research but wrote the novel's imagery and themes based on their own experiences. They wove in references to local myths, symbols, and proverbs that underscored themes of strength and belonging. Early readers praised the novel's authenticity, and the story's use of cultural elements resonated deeply with audiences, demonstrating the importance of lived cultural awareness in meaningful storytelling.

5. Thematic Cohesion: Crafting Stories with Depth and Intentionality

One of the most compelling aspects of human-authored storytelling is the ability to weave together themes and motifs in ways that create a cohesive, intentional narrative. While AI can suggest plot structures or recurring elements, it doesn't understand why certain themes—like redemption, freedom, or sacrifice—matter within a particular story context. Authors, however, use their intuition to connect themes across a narrative, giving readers an experience that feels whole and purposeful.

Example: An author writing a mystery novel might choose to echo the theme of trust throughout, using symbols like mirrors or reflections to subtly remind readers of the plot's deeper questions about perception and truth. This intentional weaving of theme and motif adds depth to the story, creating a sense of cohesion and satisfaction that AI cannot replicate.

Case Study: Crafting Stories with Depth and Intentionality

A thriller author employed AI to suggest pacing improvements but took control of thematic development to ensure that recurring symbols—such as closed doors and narrow hallways—reflected the protagonist's internal journey. These symbolic choices reinforced the story's themes of entrapment and self-discovery. Test readers found these recurring motifs added to the narrative's impact, highlighting how intentional thematic development is central to storytelling's emotional and intellectual depth.

6. Recognizing the Human Touch in Storytelling: Creativity and Originality as a Guiding Force

While AI can support technical tasks, it cannot replicate the originality and unpredictability of human creativity. Authors bring a sense of wonder, spontaneity, and inventiveness to their stories, driven by a combination of curiosity, personal reflection, and inspiration. These elements are what make literature an art form rather than a formula, providing readers with fresh, thought-provoking experiences.

Example: A sci-fi writer might be inspired to create a story based on a dream or a "what if" question that arises in their everyday life—"What if memories were currency?" AI might generate practical world-building details, but it is the author's creative vision that drives the concept, exploring themes of memory, value, and identity in unexpected ways.

Case Study: the Human Touch

A literary fiction author found themselves inspired by a chance encounter during a walk, which led to an idea for a novel about fleeting human connections. While AI helped with editing and research, the story's depth and originality emerged from the author's personal reflection on connection and loneliness. Readers connected with the story's universal themes, illustrating how spontaneous inspiration and personal insight are at the heart of meaningful storytelling.

7. Balancing AI's Strengths with Human Sensitivity and Insight

AI can be a valuable tool for enhancing productivity, refining language, and providing structural support, but its role is ultimately limited to supporting the author's creative vision. By recognizing this balance, authors can use AI as a supportive assistant without allowing it to overshadow the personal, emotional, and intuitive elements that give stories their power and meaning.

Example: An author might use AI to suggest pacing adjustments, but they rely on personal experience to decide when a scene needs more descriptive depth or when a character's vulnerability should be highlighted. This careful balance ensures that the narrative's impact comes from the author's understanding of storytelling's emotional landscape.

Case Study: **AI's Strengths and Human Sensitivity**

A YA author used AI to draft initial character profiles but shaped each character's emotional journey based on personal experiences with growth, change, and resilience. While AI helped organize and expedite the drafting process, it was the author's understanding of adolescence that gave the characters authenticity. Readers praised the book for its realistic portrayal of teenage life, showing how the human touch is essential in creating characters that resonate.

8. Embracing the Future of Storytelling: Combining AI Assistance with Human Insight

The unique value of human creativity, intuition, and emotional intelligence in storytelling remains irreplaceable, even as AI plays an increasing role in the writing process. By embracing AI as a tool rather than a replacement, authors can harness its strengths while preserving the authenticity and emotional depth that make literature meaningful. This balanced approach allows authors to explore ambitious projects, experiment with complex structures, and streamline their workflow, all while staying true to their vision.

In a future where AI continues to evolve, the role of the author will remain essential, rooted in the irreplaceable qualities of human imagination, empathy, and lived experience. Through this partnership, authors can lead the way in crafting stories that are enriched by technology yet profoundly human in their themes, insights, and emotional impact. By valuing and cultivating their unique abilities, authors ensure that storytelling continues to be an art form that resonates with readers on a deeply personal level.